The Ethnic Market
Food Guide

The Ethnic Market Food Guide

An Ingredient Encyclopedia for Cooks, Travelers, and Lovers of Exotic Food

LANE MORGAN

Another idea from becker&mayer!

BERKLEY BOOKS, NEW YORK

This book is an original publication of The Berkley Publishing Group.

THE ETHNIC MARKET FOOD GUIDE

A Berkley Book / published by arrangement with
the author

PRINTING HISTORY
Berkley trade paperback edition / November 1997

The Putnam Berkley World Wide Web site address is http://www.berkley.com

ISBN: 0-425-16130-7

BERKLEY®
Berkley Books are published by The Berkley Publishing Group,
a member of Penguin Putnam Inc.,
200 Madison Avenue, New York, New York 10016.
Berkley and the "B" design
are trademarks belonging to Berkley Publishing Corporation.

PRINTED IN THE UNITED STATES OF AMERICA

1   3   5   7   9   10   8   6   4   2

Acknowledgments

———————— ༕ ————————

Heartfelt thanks to my husband, Bruce Brown, and daughters, Laurel and Shanna, for years of taste testing, and to my intrepid shopping companions, Gretchen Hoyt and Deb Anderson-Frey. Ethlyn Hilton introduced me to the BendDown Market in Falmouth, Jamaica, and showed me how to roast a breadfruit. The staff of the Bellingham Public Library and the denizens of cookbook-1-digest, an email list, helped me locate essential references.

Thanks also to my editor, Elizabeth Beier, and my wonderful agent, Anne Depue.

Contents

———————— ❧ ————————

Introduction

My first recorded exploration into ethnic food came when I was four. My parents and I lived for a year in Mexico. One day in Oaxaca I wandered off and was found some time later by a fire pit in the park, joining a group of townsfolk in a snack of roasted grasshoppers. Since then many of my best hours have been spent learning about food in the countries I have visited. I'm particularly drawn to markets. I love the unfamiliar smells, the haggling and bantering. I would rather sample a *taquito de lengua* or try squid stuffed with "dirty rice" than go to a night-club or shop at the duty-free store. For me the best souvenirs of travel are ingredients and recipes, the smells and flavors more evocative than a photograph.

When I was eighteen I spent six months studying in Florence. The villa we students lived in was managed by an order of monks who did not believe in pampering the flesh with heat or good food. Their penury infuriated the cooks, a band of profane, chain-smoking *nonas* who felt personally implicated in the deficiencies mandated by their grocery budget. Only on Sunday did they get to cook as they saw fit. It was always the same and always wonderful: a lasagna with freshly made spinach pasta and three sauces, begun at eight A.M. and served to a hundred people twelve hours later. One Sunday a few of us spent the day in the kitchen with the old ladies, who waved their cigarettes, flirted outrageously, chased uninvited guests with cleavers, and worked with grace and confidence to show us what Tuscan food was supposed to taste like. My most treasured memento of Villa San Paolo is the recipe for that lasagna, carefully written in Italian amidst fierce argument by the cooks, splattered with tomato and cream sauce.

I also learned how cold a city made of stone can get, during a rainy winter, and how good a chunk of octopus tentacle can taste straight out of the boiling pot on a streetside table. I learned to drink good coffee and renewed my passion, developed at age seven on a trip with my parents, for hazelnut *semifreddo* ice cream.

On vacation trips, hitchhiking from the Italian campus, we considered a dollar a day a pretty fair food budget, and therefore developed an appreciative acquaintance with Greek, Yugoslav, and Turkish street food: souvlakis, *boureks, čevapčiči,* mint tea, and lots of strong sweet coffee. Occasionally as we waited for rides, families would invite us home for pilafs and roasted peppers. By budget and by inclination, I have spent more time in open-air markets than in renowned restaurants. I'm fascinated by the transformation of the cheapest, most basic ingredients into something that achieves a level beyond subsistence. My college studies in anthropology increased my interest in food in the context of culture, as an expression of hospitality and a conveyer of meaning.

In this book I have tried to share my pleasure in food and its history, the discovery of new flavors and the recreation of old favorites. I am not a professional chef. I don't have a battery of specialized cooking equipment—no pizza stone or *coucousière*—not even a microwave or a gas range (although since writing my last cookbook I have learned to use and appreciate a food processor). I'm more interested in home cooking than in recreating restaurant specialties. Anything I can do in the kitchen you surely can do in yours. Living in the country as I do, I am also a bit vague on what's the trendy cuisine of the moment. I have tried to pick ingredients and recipes for the long haul, for a lifetime of good cooking and good tastes.

In many cases, ethnic cooking is a rediscovery of foods and flavors that were papered over in North America by what one book from the 1920s called, approvingly, "Americanization through Homemaking," the attempt by middle-class reformers to rid poorer families not only of their dependence on salt pork, lard, and other high-fat, low-nutrient foods, but also of the "stimulating" influences of garlic, chiles, olive oil, and other flavorful favorites of immigrant households. The English ethnic background of most of the reformers meant that the reference points for proper cooking were white sauces rather than moles and marinaras, a joint of beef rather than a stir-fried squid or a bowl of *menudo*. In the process of this "Americanization," many families also lost track of true American specialties. Anxious hostesses in the Pacific Northwest would bypass their own incomparable salmon to serve duck *à l'orange* and Southern cooks chose mock turtle soup over their own gumbo. Of course, some brave souls always did resist these culinary insecurities and continued to serve their ethnic and regional specialties. And in recent decades, more tourism and new waves of immigration have brought the cuisines of the world to our consciousness and our kitchens as never before.

Although novelty attracts us to new cuisines, the enduring strength of any cooking is in its basics, the appetites that are daily satisfied and daily renewed. As we explore a new kind of cooking we can try to keep both worlds in mind—the simple daily satisfaction of feeding friends and family, and the inspirations of a highly developed food tradition. The time I've spent researching and preparing the ingredients in this book has given me glimpses of both.

How This Book Works

Most of the ingredients in your favorite ethnic restaurants are going to be available in your community. After all, the chefs have to buy that food somewhere. Shopping for ingredients you're not used to may be daunting, however. How do you choose among a dozen colors of dal when all the names are in Punjabi? How do you work backward from the perfectly sliced and seasoned vegetables in a Thai soup to the lumpy tubers piled in a box on the sidewalk? How green should a green mango be? The aim of this book is to take some of the confusion and guesswork, but not the adventure, out of trying new ingredients and new dishes. Cooking ethnic dishes at home also gives you a chance to try a much wider range of dishes. Restaurant meals tend to represent just a fraction of the cooking styles of their native cuisines. They inevitably favor dishes that cook up in a hurry (hence the preponderance of stir fries in Chinese restaurants) or that can handle reheating. They may be concentrated for cultural reasons on one regional cuisine (Northern Indian, for example) in a country of tremendous culinary diversity. Neighborhood ethnic markets, on the other hand, will sell what ordinary families eat for breakfast, lunch, and dinner.

This book has three major parts: the basics of distinctive world cuisines (obscenely abbreviated), a descriptive listing of foods, and an annotated resource list of some of my favorite cookbooks.

The list of ingredients is presented alphabetically by each item's best-known common name. It contains a description of each ingredient's looks, taste and uses, shopping information, possible substitutions, and in some cases a representative recipe. This is not a cookbook and we couldn't provide a recipe for every ingredient, so we have also included recipe references. For these, I have tried to choose books that are readily available in stores or at the library.

I feel a bit uneasy with culinary globetrotting, as much as I enjoy it. Food is one of our great opportunities for understanding culture, but those insights take time and attention. We may miss out on this connection if we are always in search of the newest flavor—Yucatecan one night, Cambodian the next. However, there is a corresponding advantage when one starts to trace ingredients and cooking ideas from one continent to another. Given the same basic ingredients, different cooks will come up with both a wonderful diversity of interpretation and a common bond. A Greek candied eggplant and a Chinese eggplant in black bean sauce are so different as to seem two entirely different foodstuffs. But a **pepian de chumpipe** from the Mayan village of Huehuetenango in the Guatemalan highlands, with turkey simmered in a spicy sauce thickened with ground seeds, shares the same culinary inspiration as a chicken *korma* from the Moghul palaces of India. These linkages are sometimes historical, as in the clear trail of foods and techniques transmitted in the African diaspora, and sometimes the independent inspirations of culinary minds addressing the same challenges.

How to Shop

You can get what's needed for many ethnic dishes at the simplest local supermarket just by knowing what to look for. Cream of Wheat is farina, albeit doctored a bit with preservatives and salt, and that means you are ready to make India's most popular home dessert, *sooji halwa.* Regular brown lentils can make excellent dal, as long as you have the right recipe. With lemons and salt and a few days' time, you can have *hamed m'raked,* one of the most characteristic and exotic flavorings of Moroccan cuisine. Korean kimchee is as close as that pile of Chinese cabbage in the produce section. Still, the time will come when you need ingredients beyond what the corner store supplies. A well-stocked upscale supermarket will have many of them, especially for the current trends. Food co-ops are another good source, especially for unusual grains and flours, and for the Japanese foods that can be used in macrobiotic diets. But the best-stocked and most interesting selections are naturally from the specialty markets in immigrant and ethnic communities. That's where you get an idea what an Indian or a Vietnamese kitchen should smell like. That's also where you will find the best prices. Housewives who cook with basmati rice daily are not going to pay gourmet prices to buy it one pound at a time. I get mine at the "stop-n-shop" section of our small town's Sikh-run gas station and I pay sixty cents a pound. It costs twice that in the gourmet section of the supermarket. I know that some shoppers find ethnic markets a bit intimidating, and I hope this book will ease the way.

Some ethnic food stores, like Seattle's famous Asian supermarket Uwajimaya, are as carefully laid out and gleamingly high-tech as the most upscale supermarket chain. Many are designed as much for tourists as for their local communities. But many of my favorites are more like governments in exile—a little disorganized, a little suspicious of outsiders, havens for the homesick. If you have fond memories of shopping in village markets in other countries, you will feel right at home. Otherwise you may be in for a bit of a shock. Labels may not be in English. Proprietors may give priority to their regular customers and ignore you entirely. Also, standards of hygiene may not be exactly what the USDA had in mind. Cans of intriguing pickled vegetables may be long past their "best sold by" dates. Packaged seasonings and cosmetic hair oils may be side by side on the shelves, a bit disconcerting if you can't read the labels and aren't sure whether an ingredient is supposed to be eaten or rubbed on.

Outside of the very occasional buggy batch of imported grains (which I now forestall by keeping them in the freezer), I have never had a problem with the food I've bought in ethnic groceries being spoiled or otherwise unwholesome, and my strong advice is to take things as you find them. If you don't want to buy from a bulk bin that someone else has been rummaging through to get the choicest pieces, then don't. But don't wrinkle your nose and complain to the management. You will also be a better customer and have a better time if you do a little homework before you buy. Even a modestly informed question usually brings an outpouring of help and information from proprietors and fellow shoppers. Everything I know about Jamaican curry mutton and the Punjabi ways with dal I learned at the checkout counters of local markets, when the proprietors sternly asked me if I knew how to cook what I had bought.

Scope of This Book

No food reference book can be completely comprehensive, and this one makes no claim to be all-inclusive. I have tried to concentrate on ingredients that are versatile and that are available in North America; I have left out, for example, some luscious tropical fruits that don't travel well. I have favored grains and seasonings over meat and produce, on the theory that they are the most distinctive flavors of a cuisine and the ingredients that may require the most guidance. I also concentrated on ingredients less likely to be covered in standard general cookbooks; hence the short shrift given to many essential and characteristic European foods. For example, I have listed kimchee but not sauerkraut, though each is essential to its homeland cooks. This is not meant to say that Korea is more "ethnic" than Germany, but simply to provide the most help possible within a limited number of pages.

In addition to the specific variety listings, you will find brief general discussions on widespread foods such as vinegars, olives, noodles, and chiles. These are intended to help you plan substitutions for less available ingredients and to learn the general properties of some of the world's most popular foods.

If you want to see a truly heroic effort to list and explain all ethnic ingredients, check your local library or bookstore for *The von Welanetz Guide to Ethnic Ingredients*. It has more listings, more recipes, and more detail than you will find here. But even its more than 700 large and jam-packed pages do not cover everything, and new foods are now being imported to North America all the time. I hope this book will be comprehensive enough to be useful, yet compact enough to be accessible.

There is a lot of disagreement and a fair amount of misinformation in food books, especially with newly trendy cuisines where the urge to profit on popularity sometimes outstrips the desire to get it right. One best-selling series I consulted informed me that "the cocoa tree yields chocolate from its nut and cocaine from its leaves," thereby giving a whole new meaning to the term *chocoholic*. (It's not true, folks.) I have purchased and cooked with most of the ingredients in this book. In a few cases where I couldn't obtain an important ingredient, I have tried to cross-check each assertion with more than one reliable source. Any errors remaining are my responsibility.

Part One

&

World Cuisines

Sub-Saharan Africa

Picture a summer table. A platter of grilled chicken waits next to a bowl of its dipping sauce, a bright combination of fresh mint, cilantro, ground roasted peanuts, chile peppers, garlic, and lime juice. Avocado halves are stuffed with a salad of hard-boiled eggs, flakes of smoked fish, and sweet pepper, moistened with lime juice and coconut milk. A rosy pink oval of something that looks like polenta soaks up the juices from a dish of cold fish and shrimp, marinated in a spicy mixture of tomato, vinegar, and vegetables. Little crispy wheat crackers, like miniature breadsticks, turn out to be hot enough to send the casual muncher over to the iced mint tea or the beer.

The cuisine of sub-Saharan Africa is probably the least known in North America. With the exception of the distinctive dishes of Ethiopia—tangy cottage cheese with greens, huge

11

spongy rounds of *injera* bread made from teff, long-cooked curries of chicken and goat—few African restaurants are found here. And unlike Europe and Asia, Africa does not have the legacy of generations of travelers coming back to America with fond memories of great cooking. On the contrary, in many countries one of the legacies of African colonialism is a tradition of truly awful restaurant food, summed up by Rhodesian-born writer Doris Lessing as "vast meals which must be among the worst offered to suffering humanity anywhere." Laurens van der Post writes that for generations the only book published on East African cooking was *The Kenya Settlers Cookery Book and Household Guide*, which contains both haggis and "mock-haggis" but barely a passing reference to native African food or techniques. In a region of superb stovetop stews and complex sauces, it recommends flavoring stock with bouillon cubes. Needless to say, this is not the food that most Africans eat.

For most Americans, the closest brush with West African cooking comes with the "soul food" of the South. The jambalayas and gumbos of Louisiana, mixing seafood, vegetables, and poultry and thickened with okra (an African import, as is the term *gumbo*), would taste familiar from Nigeria to Sierra Leone. Unlike the willing immigrants who planned their journeys, slaves arriving in the Americas were seldom able to bring treasured seeds or ingredients with them, but some transplants did arrive—including peanuts, cumin, and sesame, still called by its African name of *benne* in the American South—and homesick Africans learned to adapt their dishes to the foods available in the new country. Gumbos, fritters, spoon breads, greens, and "pot likker" all show the hallmarks of traditional West African cooking. Masters who marveled at their slaves' talent in the kitchen did not stop to think that they were dealing not with an instinctive gift but with skills developed from long experience. Soul food exemplifies many of the basics of present-day African cooking—bold combinations of fish, meat, and poultry; a frequent base of tomato, hot pepper, and onion; stews, patties, and other soft textures as opposed to crisp, separate flavors; and well-flavored slow-cooked greens.

Favorite Caribbean and South American dishes, especially those from Brazil, also clearly show their African origin. Salt fish and ackee, the national dish of Jamaica, has the hallmarks of West African cooking, and the toasted cassava powder and palm oil that characterize much of the zesty cooking of the Bahia region of Brazil is equally popular in Lagos. In fact, Brazilian slaves who repatriated to Nigeria brought with them the Latin American tradition of a marinade of chiles, onion, and citrus used to "cook" raw fish, introducing a cooking genre called *imoyo* to West Africa.

The introduction of tomatoes, capiscum peppers, and corn to Africa from the West made changes in favored dishes, but the basics of West African cooking remained the same, and remain so still: a large serving of a bland carbohydrate, whether cassava or yam or, more recently, rice, served with bites of a spicy stew or stewed vegetables. The documentary image of village women pounding grain by the hour in a giant mortar is a testament to the central place of this starchy centerpiece, generically known as *fufu*, in African diets. Now instant *fufu* is available in bar-coded packages in the West: just add water. On the coasts and rivers, and among the middle class, a distinctive cuisine based on grilled fish has developed. The fish may be marinated in lemon juice and spices, and then basted while cooking with a mixture of palm oil and peppers.

Another characteristic that has not changed is the centrality of food and hospitality in African culture. Because food is often scarce and sharing it is a cultural imperative, African meals tend not to be doled out in single courses. A typical West African meal consists of a rich stew with a bit of chicken or fish, often with a breathtaking quantity of orange palm oil, eaten with a dish of one of the staples—cassava, yams, cowpeas ("the poor man's meat"), or millet in nontropical areas. The traditional serving style is to put the main dish into individual plates and the porridge or loaf into a common serving dish. Each diner plucks a lump of porridge or loaf, shapes it with thumb and forefinger so it is slightly oval and hollowed like a spoon, then dips and turns it in the stew and swallows the morsel whole.

In the herding regions of East Africa, a distinctive cuisine has developed that makes more use of dairy products. A smattering of Ethiopian restaurants have introduced North Americans to some of the flavors of East African cooking, where tiny-seeded teff is the predominant grain, used to make the sourish, spongy bread *injera*. Dairy products are also more common in the drier East, leading to delicate flavorings such as the spiced butter *nitter kibbeh*, and the distinctive Ethiopian cottage cheese. Laurens van der Post describes the traditional peasant meal of *tedj*, a mead made from the intensely flavored honey of the

Ethiopian highlands; cottage cheese; and *injera* with honey-
comb as evoking the essence of East Africa, both basic and refined. Less to his taste but also representative is the meal of raw
meat dipped into *berbere* sauce, common to warriors and other
travelers who have no time for husbandry. The Ethiopian Christian tradition, which requires frequent meatless days, has led—
in the communities that can afford it—to an inventive series of
vegetable and grain-based dishes, including the famous fried
"fish" formed of garbanzo flour, and many vegetable *wats*, or
stews, featuring the strong flavors of African greens, best approximated by collards. Roasted camel hump, giraffe marrow
bones, and hippopotamus lard, other traditional East African
foods of the plains further south, are unlikely to reach the West.

Southern Africa has the largest European presence, as well as
separate "coloured" communities of South Asian descent. Curries, chutneys, Malaysian boboties and bredies, and Afrikaans
milk tarts and beet salads are all characteristic.

African cooking is a stovetop or more commonly firetop af-
fair, with baking a relatively recent addition. Except for fish,
meat is generally both scarce and tough, so marinades, small
pieces, and simmered stews all suit both the product and the
process. Produce is generally homegrown, although the packaged *fufus* and other foodstuffs lighten the burden of preparing
food, at least for city cooks.

For newcomers to African food, the standard stews and *fufus*
of West African cooking may not be the best introduction.
Much traditional West African food, though savory and inventive, is frankly gloppy. Thickeners like *egusi* and okra, combined

with lots of strongly flavored palm oil, create flavors and textures that take some getting used to. It may be best to begin with the grilled fish and chicken dishes and their spicy chutneylike sauces, and to substitute rice for the more common cassava and yam.

Beer, either commercially brewed or homemade, probably is the most common drink, and much African beer is very good. Tea and herbal drinks are important in the Moslem countries, which do not endorse alcohol. In South Africa, the combination of good farmland and a British tradition has led to the production of some excellent brandy.

You may well not find an African food market in your community, and when you do it's just as likely to be tucked away in some unlikely neighborhood. In my experience the staff is likely to be extremely friendly and supportive of your interest in this little-known cuisine, which is good, because many of the African imports have cryptic labels (or none at all) and no instructions. Caribbean, Latin American, and Asian markets will carry many of the ingredients you need, such as palm oil, cassava, and yam.

Latin America/South America/The Caribbean

For anyone whose experience stops with fajitas and margaritas at the local CalMex eatery, the complexity and variety of traditional Mexican cuisine alone is overwhelming, and South American and Caribbean cooking are equally diverse.

≈§ MEXICO The basic foods of Mexico—the corn, beans, and chiles of every Mexican restaurant anywhere—are familiar to all. For visitors to Mexico the real food is often a big surprise on several counts. One is that unlike the cheese-soaked combo plates of your local corner spot, Mexican dishes tend to have clean, distinct flavors: Sliced fruit is served with chile powder and lemon juice. A freshly made blue-corn tortilla is wrapped around a bit of sautéed zucchini and a bit of crumbled white *queso fresco,* not a swamp of orange grease. The other surprise is the tremendous variety of regional cuisines using the corn/bean base. Mexico is a huge country, to an extent often unappreciated if you have only hit the Pacific Coast resorts, and is varied both geographically and ethnically. Recipes in Guanajuato may have a strong Spanish influence; those in the Yucatán use ground pumpkin seeds and the indigenous herb *epazote* for flavors never imagined in Europe. The names sometimes give a clue as to origin. *Tacos de requesón* are Spanish, with lime, ricotta, and radishes in addition to the native cilantro and corn. *Dzotobichay,* a Yucatecan tamale, has retained its Mayan name and is probably unchanged since before European contact. The moles and salsas of Mexico (there are seven famous moles in Oaxaca alone) are at least as varied as the regional sauces of France, though less celebrated. Diana Kennedy provides recipes for more than thirty in *The Art of Mexican Cooking,* with no claims of being comprehensive.

Mexican beers are justly famous, and the tequila and mescal is the stuff of legends. However, perhaps because I lived there as a child, my memories are of the other drinks: hot chocolate spiced with cinnamon, *café con leche* eaten with pan dulce, milky sweet *horchatas,* and the ubiquitous *liquados,* combining fresh fruit, eggs, milk, and ice to make a divine sort of Papaya (or Melon, or Mango) Julius.

CENTRAL AMERICA Pumpkin seeds, squash, tomatoes, peppers, and sometimes a bit of poultry or pork give variety to the basic corn and beans of the Central American highlands. Even eggs are precious and not used lightly. In *The Jaguar's Smile,* a fascinating little book on Nicaragua under the Sandinistas, Salman Rushdie describes a village meal: "With the generosity of the poor, they treated me to a delicacy at lunch. I was given an egg and bean soup, the point being that these eggs were the best-tasting, because they had been fertilized. Such eggs were known as 'the eggs of love.' " One of the characteristic techniques of indigenous Central American cooking, *pepian,* is well worth trying. Meat, usually chicken or turkey, is first boiled in plain water and then cooked in a sauce thickened with ground seeds and enlivened with chile. Other strands of Central American cooking are the very European dishes of the bigger cities and the African/Caribbean influence of the eastern seacoast.

SOUTH AMERICA Like many regions with a colonial past, South America has several distinct food traditions. There just isn't much culinary common ground between an ethnic Italian townhouse dweller in Buenos Aires, eating ravioli and looking out over the Atlantic (there is an old joke: What did the Argentine say when he went to Rome and first saw an Italian phone book? "I had no idea so many Argentines lived here") and a Quechua potato grower near Lake Titicaca. Much of the cuisine of the urban middle class still harks back to the "old country," and much of the indigenous food is aimed at the most basic level of survival. And, like Africa, South America has failed to attract the kind of tourist traffic that brings back a demand for its best dishes. But there are exceptions. The Brazilian cuisine of the Bahia, an adventurous mixture of Portuguese, African, and indigenous people, is as memorable as you are likely to find anywhere. *Moqueca de peixe* (see recipe under **Palm nut oil**) is one example, combining the escabeche technique of Portugal with African palm oil and South American coconut in a splendid seafood dish. Another Brazilian favorite, feijoada, is a mixture of colonial and indigenous tastes, combining black beans, local greens, chiles, tomatoes, and cassava meal—all regional natives—with corned beef and other European introductions.

Even at their plainest, the native potato varieties of the Bolivian and Peruvian highlands are another revelation in color and taste. Andean families dry huge quantities of potatoes, which store easily in the dry cold air. Less subsistence-oriented cooks will be more interested in fresh potato recipes, which give full credit to the incomparable flavor of fingerling potatoes. Interest in these ancient varieties has been resurging, and farmers' markets and specialty groceries offer an ever-growing selection of "purple Peruvians" and other small, delicious, "unimproved" types.

Corn is not as basic in South America as it is in Central America, but is still important, and is often found in thicker, more pancake-like skillet breads than the more familiar tortillas. Quinoa and amaranth, two cold-hardy seed crops, may take the place of corn in the harsh climate of the *altiplano*. In the cattle-raising areas of Argentina and Chile, the diet is not dissimilar to the classic North American steak and potatoes, with one well-known diversion: the popular herbal tea maté. Chile and Argentina have the climate and traditions to maintain fine vineyards, and their wines are beginning to have an impact on the export market.

❧ THE CARIBBEAN African, Amerindian, East Indian, Dutch, French, Spanish, and British influences all crowd together in the Caribbean. This worldwide blend of cultures, a tropical extravagance of produce and seafood, and the relative isolation of island communities have led to an amazing variety of distinctive and delicious foods. Returning tourists and West Indian émigrés have popularized some dishes, especially the spicy, tangy marinade that produces Jamaica's famous jerk pork and chicken.

In these primarily black countries, dishes and techniques imported from Africa have a much more obvious influence even than in the American South. Both cultures like black-eyed peas, but in the Caribbean black-eyed pea fritters, called *calla* or *akkra*, are virtually identical to those served in Nigeria, except for the use of vegetable oil rather than palm oil. Salt fish, another African and European staple, shows up in dozens of forms, my favorite being the Jamaican salt fish and ackee (another African transplant). *Fufus* and other starchy basics also have traveled nearly unchanged between Africa and the islands.

European traditions meet island produce in a fascinating synthesis of flavors. Pudding and souse, an inter-island classic, would be familiar enough in Holland, except for the island touch of marinating the pork hocks with lime juice. Dishes featuring Dutch cheeses are another island translation, such as *kesy yena (queso relleno)*, in which a whole Edam or Gouda cheese is stuffed with beef or shrimp, tomatoes, olives, onion, and some island hot peppers. Some of the world's hottest peppers grow on the islands, and are used inventively to spark the bland carbohydrate staples of cassava and cornmeal, or the ubiquitous rice and peas. Caribbean hot sauces are as common and as varied as Mexican salsas. Generally they have a generous amount of vinegar or lime.

Seafood, including the famously mild and prolific conch, is often served in *escovitch*, a spicy, vinegared sauce that is a close cousin to seviche. Island land crabs, which spend most of the year as garden pests, undermining plantings, chewing up roots, and generally filling the role of moles or prairie dogs on the mainland, get the same treatment during their harvest season.

When it comes to beverages, the Caribbean is nearly synonymous with rum, but there is plenty else to drink, including several excellent local beers. On the English-speaking islands tea is a standard, so much so that the name adheres to all hot drinks, as in "coffee tea," traditionally taken with condensed milk and lots of sugar. Jamaica's famous Blue Mountain coffee is probably easier to find in North America than on the islands, as most of the crop goes for export. Another island specialty, also popular in Mexico, is a ruby-colored iced tea of tart hibiscus flowers, known locally as *sorrel* but in other countries as *Jamaica*.

Most supermarkets sell an increasing selection of Mexican food. My local market has graduated from refried beans and taco shells to *menudo* and dried *camarones*. Caribbean specialties are less likely to appear on the regular grocery shelves, but specialty markets should be able to sell you everything but the delicate fresh fruits and indigenous seafoods.

Southeast Asia

Common threads of Southeast Asian cooking include coconut; fresh coriander; citrus flavors from leaves, peel, and fruit, as well as the milder taste of lemongrass; and the ever-present undercurrents of dried or fermented fish and shellfish. The region is the native home of the chicken, which is second in popularity to seafood. Chiles, especially hot ones, have been welcomed with enthusiasm for their contrast and complements to the richness of coconut milk and the bright tastes of ginger and galangal. The cooking in general is very light and often very sophisticated, with carefully balanced flavors of coconut, vinegar, chile, and ginger. Compared with Western cooking (and with restaurants in the Western world), Asian food involves a lot more rice and a lot less of what restaurant goers consider the "main courses." Most meals consist of several dishes, all served together rather than in separate courses. Soup is sipped throughout the meal, serving as both a beverage and another dish.

In Vietnam the long French occupation has yielded a legacy of French breads, pastries, and pâtés, which blend well with the carefully composed soups and salads of the indigenous cuisines. Laotian and Cambodian food is similar, but is distinguished in part by the reliance on fresh fish rather than saltwater fish, and in part by a preference for glutinous rice as the primary staple. Thai cooking is additionally famous for its curries, some of them Indian in provenance and others characteristically Southeast Asian.

KOREA Seattle got its first Korean restaurant in 1962, a by-product of the World's Fair of that year, and I became an instant convert. I loved the rich surprising taste of cold marinated spinach with sesame seeds, and I was taken with the glamour of the gleaming metal chopsticks, so much more impressive to a child than plain wooden ones. I was crazy about *bulgoki*—thin cuts of beef, marinated and charcoal grilled. It was a long time before my experience advanced further, but eventually I learned more about Korean cooking and it still is one of my favorites.

Korea is a peninsula, with limited arable land and some of the most severe weather in Asia. It is not surprising, then, that seafood predominates its cuisine, and hearty flavors are favored over some of the delicately balanced, appetite-teasing dishes of the tropics. The need for preserving scarce food over the winter has led to a huge array of dried and pickled dishes. Kimchee is the best known, but is only one of many assertive flavors. "For centuries, the staple diet of the ordinary Korean has consisted of rice, dried or pickled fish, pickled vegetables and precious little else," writes Marc Mellon in *Flavours of Korea*. Even so, a standard meal is likely to consist of as many as a dozen dishes, with several varieties of kimchee and more than one seafood tidbit. Korean grocers stock an amazing assortment of dried vegetables, including dried sweet-potato stems, dried green-pepper leaves, dried sliced radish, dried lotus root, dried garlic stems, and dried sea mustard stems—as well as their fresh produce.

Unlike most Asian countries, Korea favors beef over other meats as in *bulgoki* and *yukhoe,* in which the beef is marinated and eaten raw. Pork is more common in the mountainous north, which lacks much pasture, and seafood, both fresh and dried, is popular everywhere.

Noodles are second only to rice as a staple, and Korea also has invented favorites that are little known outside the country—a porridge made of ground pine nuts, for example, and a sort of tofu made from acorns. It's a great place for substantial, warming street food—steamed mussels on the half shell, rice cakes in chile sauce, onion pancakes, and sweet-potato french fries.

Many Korean immigrants to the United States have found a niche running small groceries; it's worth checking there for specialty foods, even if their main fare is beer and snacks. Otherwise look for specialty ethnic markets. When it comes to kimchee, the most characteristic of all Korean flavors, most well-stocked supermarkets now carry it, and it is not difficult to make your own.

🍃 PHILIPPINES Coconut milk, shrimp paste, sweet and sticky desserts, and tangy sweet-and-sour adobo marinades are characteristic of Philippine food, an inventive mixture of Malayan, Chinese, Japanese, Spanish, and American cuisines. The best-known Philippine dishes outside the islands are of Chinese origin, such as *lumpia* (a variety of spring roll) and *pancit* noodles, although adobo, another favorite, is an indigenous invention. Ginataan dishes—seafood, vegetables, or fruit desserts less well known in the United States—are cooked in coconut milk in the Malaysian tradition. In general, there are fewer spices and a less subtle balance of flavors than in most other Asian food traditions, but the Philippines comprise thousands of islands and many different cultures, so a northern Catholic community's favorite pork *binagoongang*—pork spareribs with shrimp paste—would be shunned in the predominantly Muslim south, both for the prohibited pork and because it lacks enough hot peppers to interest a palate heavily influenced by South Indian cooking. A more likely dish there would be *hipon sa gata,* prawns simmered in coconut milk spiced with chiles. One island favorite that you are unlikely to encounter on a North American restaurant menu is *balut*—cooked eggs containing the partially developed embryo, known in some circles as "Eggs with Legs." I have not tried these and cannot advise you further.

🍃 CHINA Chinese cooking is one of the oldest and least written down (until recently) of all great cuisines. For most Chinese the main issue has always been simply getting enough to eat. In that quest every possible food source has been explored, from jellyfish to predatory birds. Affluent households have been able to concentrate on a harmonious balance of flavors and textures, which has always been more important to Chinese cooks than any specific listing of ingredients. The Five Flavors—bitter, sour, hot, salt and sweet—were established as a goal for the cooking in wealthy kitchens more than 2,000 years ago, providing a link to other numerical guidelines in Chinese life. Chinese cooking probably also involves more metaphorical associations and cosmological links than any other cuisine, certainly more than with American food (with the possible exception of that neighborhood potluck standby, Sex in a Pan). Many dishes carry a weight of associations to which outsiders are largely oblivious and to which names like *Braised Triple White* or *Pork of Original Preciousness* carry only a clue. Noodles represent long life because of their own length. "Scallions were chung and they were to be considered wise because the character for 'wise' translates as chung ming," writes Eileen Yin-Fei Lo in *From the Earth: Chinese Vegetarian Cooking.* "And why were they wise? Because scallions are long and hollow, and their hollowness connotes an open mind, open to knowledge, receptive to thought." Even the simplest dish may exist on several levels—color contrasts, cosmological significance, homophonic resonance, contrasts and balances of size and texture. This may be daunting to the home cook, but in fact you can't go too far wrong if you stick with the fundamental principles of Chinese cooking—to use each ingredient at the peak of its flavor and to plan its associations carefully. Chinese cooking tends to have lots of little ingredients and table condiments, but few spices.

The types of heating—generally stir-frying, steaming, and braising—are carefully studied and applied to draw maximum flavor.

Cantonese cooking is the most subtle of the Chinese regional styles, has the most affluent tradition (accounting for delicacies like bird's-nest soup and shark-fin soup), and has been the most influenced by foreign traders. It also has long been the most mistreated in North America, as the majority of nineteenth-century immigrants were Cantonese and did not come trained as chefs. The first North American Chinese restaurants were established out of necessity to feed wifeless workers and had to make do with unskilled chefs and unfamiliar ingredients, which have passed on to us uninspired dishes such as chop suey. Floppy, overcooked vegetables in gloppy cornstarch sauce, or fluorescent sweet-and-sour, made me think for years that I didn't like Cantonese food, and some of that opprobrium has stuck even with the advent of wonderful Cantonese restaurants. Canton has the most favorable growing conditions in China and its dishes make use of a tremendous variety of vegetables and fruits, all treated with respect and presented at their peak of flavor. Cantonese cooking uses little seasoning, so there are no disguises for inferior ingredients or careless preparation.

Shanghai and Cantonese dishes are somewhat similar, coming from a similar climate, but they tend to be more strongly flavored—the sweets more sweet and the sours more sour. Rice is the staple. Pork, chicken, and seafood are the meats, and red sauces, strongly flavored with soy sauce and slowly braised, are popular. *Siu loon bau,* a dumpling filled with jellied pork and shrimp soup that reliquefies when heated to give the tastebuds a surprise, is a typical Shanghai production. It gains further interest from its local accompaniment of shredded ginger and red vinegar dipping sauce.

Northern Chinese cooking, often given the misleading Mandarin label in the West, uses more wheat than rice—the pancakes in *mu shu* pork, the steamed buns and pancakes, and the wrappings for spring rolls. It also uses more lamb and mutton, especially among the sparsely populated areas of Mongolia and Manchuria, and richer, heavier flavors such as black bean sauce and dark soy sauce.

Sichuan (or Szechwan) cooking makes the most use of that relative latecomer to China, the chile, as well as the native Sichuan pepper, a different plant and flavor altogether. It has lots of smoked and barbecued meats and poultry and many deep-fried dishes. Sichuan is also the home of one of my all-time favorites, hot and sour soup. Hunan cooking is similar, but hotter, using lots of chile pastes as well as whole chiles. *Kung pao* chicken, a Chinese restaurant staple, is Hunanese.

Fukien cooking is particularly well known for soups, which may be one reason that it is not so well known outside of China. A Fukien menu could contain several soups—some thick, some thin, some sweet, some savory—a combination that does not translate well to American eating habits.

China, like India, has a long vegetarian tradition based on religion (as distinguished from the world's millions who are primarily vegetarian by necessity). The Buddhist proscriptions against killing or eating meat (with the exceptions of mussels, clams, and oysters) have led to inventive dishes based on the myriad forms of soy protein and on wheat gluten. Taoists also generally avoid meat. Unlike India's vegetarian cooking, which makes no pretense to be anything else, Chinese dishes often make teasing references to the missing meat. Dishes named *Buddha's Duck* or *Buddha's Chicken* may be created to mimic the look, though not the flavor, of the original.

Chinese markets can be a bit overwhelming for the uninitiated. There are so many choices of ingredients and often very few clues in English. Although I generally love to simply browse among unfamiliar foods and buy as the spirit moves me, in Chinatown I try to take a list and follow it. I don't want to come home with a collection of disconnected ingredients that will never fulfill my goal of a harmonious balance.

❧ JAPAN Japan's relatively homogeneous population has resulted in fewer regional cuisines than in China or India, but an equal disparity between the robust dishes of everyday life and the highly refined, restrained foods for elegant and ceremonial occasions. Still the differences are no doubt less shocking to us than to the eleventh-century Kyoto court lady Sei Shonagon, who after a lifetime of the subtlest refinements of Japanese cuisine, had her first sight of hungry workers at a table:

> The moment the food was brought, they fell on the soup bowls and gulped down the contents. Then they pushed the bowls aside and polished off all the vegetables. I was wondering whether they were going to leave their rice; a second later there wasn't a grain left in their bowls. They

all behaved in exactly the same way and I suppose this must be the nature of carpenters.

Today, rich, savory stews of chicken and taro, or oysters and miso, contrast with soups consisting of a few whole shrimp, some leaves of mitsuba, and clear, subtly flavored fish stock, the essential dashi. Soups are basic to Japanese meals, served at every meal including breakfast. Street food often consists of a bowl of ramen, slurped while standing at a sidewalk counter.

Although Japanese beef is world renowned, seafood is the most important animal protein by far. Soybeans are the other essential protein source, and no other country has found more ways to use them, in shoyu, miso, natto, and tofu in its dozens of elaborations.

The preferred rice is medium grain and should be fresh—as opposed, for example, to basmati, which is believed to improve with age. Japanese cooks wash rice thoroughly first, especially for sushi, which must not have any gummy starch coating to interfere with the purity of flavor. Unlike Indian and most American rice recipes, you start out cooking Japanese rice in cold water and use only a little more water than rice.

Although its reputation as a healthful, low-fat cuisine is deserved, Japanese cooking also involves a lot of sugar, to glaze vegetables and moderate the saltiness of soy sauce, and considerable use of deep-fat frying. The contrasts between the light soups, tangy pickled vegetables, snowy rice, and the crisp outsides and tender centers of a standard tempura dinner, though not particularly adventurous dining, are a fair representation of the visual and culinary balances of this cuisine.

In contrast to many other ethnic markets, Japanese groceries tend toward meticulous organization and lots of packaging. Foods may be unrecognizable, but they are shrink wrapped and bar coded. If you are lucky, you have a store in the vicinity that sells fresh *omochi* rice pastries, and you can experience one of the true indigenous tastes of Japan, sweet and subtle and beautifully balanced.

✅ INDONESIA With nearly 20,000 islands and 300 ethnic groups, Indonesia has a bewildering variety of food traditions, linked together in general by the reliance on rice (except on Ambon, where the staple is sago, and on Irian Jaya, where it's sweet potato) and coconut. Rice accompanied by one or two vegetable side dishes and one or two condiments is a typical meal. Seafood, freshwater fish, and chicken are the main protein sources, as well as the soy product tempeh when meat isn't available. Indonesian chickens tend to be muscular, backyard birds, so they are often boiled and then barbecued, the first for tenderness and the second for flavor.

The real magic in Indonesian cuisine is in the use of aromatic seasonings: fresh shallots, fresh garlic, fresh green onions, fresh rhizomes such as ginger and its galangal cousins, and fresh turmeric. Lemongrass and kaffir lime, essential to Thai food, are also important here, as are the dried spices of coriander seeds, cardamom, cinnamon or cassia, cumin, and fennel. Surprisingly, nutmeg, cloves, and mace, spices that first brought traders to Indonesia to make their fortunes, appear seldom. Along with the aromatics go rich sweet coconut milk, palm sugar, and *kecap manis* (a sweetened soy sauce), moderated by tamarind, lime juice, and vinegar. Ground candlenuts, rather than flour, are used as thickeners, and pastries tend to be made from rice flour, fried or steamed, rather than wheat.

The best-known Indonesian food outside of Indonesia is no doubt the *ristaffel*, a tableful of rice and side dishes that actually is a legacy of Dutch colonialism. Satays, where chicken, shrimp, or more rarely, beef, is grilled and served with peanut sauce, are better representations of what Indonesians actually cook at home.

While many of the specialty vegetables and fruits used in Indonesian cooking are not available in the United States, most of the herbs and spices that provide the signature flavors can be found in Southeast Asian markets. Even candlenuts, which until recently were not found on this continent, are now on sale here.

~ INDIA India is so large and so diverse a country, both in climate and in culture, that it is probably stupid to attempt any generalizations about its food. Even the restricted range of dishes generally found in Indian restaurants (not only in North America but in India itself) offers impressive variety, and that barely scratches the surface. The foods most familiar to restaurant goers are from the North Indian Punjabi cuisines. Restaurateur and cookbook author Camella Panjabi explains that Punjabis are the most mobile ethnic group both within and outside India and the most attuned to eating out. Also, their menus, which allow meat, are more familiar to the average omnivorous North American diner. So although tandoori chicken, which requires a special oven, is prepared in only a fraction of Indian homes, it has come to represent Indian cooking in the minds of many aficionados.

Most Indian cooking is influenced by the ancient Ayurvedic precepts of health and diet, which divide food by its tastes—sweet, sour, salty, bitter, pungent, astringent—and its effects on the body and spirit. All the tastes must be present and balanced in a meal to promote health. Further, the nature of food corresponds to levels of personality, so that fresh, lightly cooked, easily digestible food contributes to a pure nature, concerned with understanding life and dealing with it fairly. Highly spiced foods and those from slaughtered animals contribute to a less sensitive, more dominating personality, while oily, overcooked, or stale food (think fast-food french fries here) contribute to the lowest, dullest traits. Thus a high-caste Brahmin will avoid the highly spiced foods often associated with Indian cuisine in favor of subtly flavored *kormas*.

Kashmiri food is hearty, as befits the mountainous climate, with a distinctive, mildly hot Kashmiri pepper and considerable use of fennel flavoring. Turnips and lamb, the sort of ingredients you might expect in Greece or Bulgaria, are given a distinctive treatment here. Kashmiri cooking also shares elements with Iranian cuisine, as in a *kofta* made of minced lamb that echoes the Arab way with spiced meatballs. The cooking of

Zoroastrian Parsi communities also shows Iranian influences, including the combination of meat and fruit exemplified by a dish of sweet and sour curried lamb with apricots.

Moghul food is characterized by the use of nuts, often almonds, and by aromatic rather than hot spices such as saffron and *kewra*. Some of these are the fabled court dishes of the Indian aristocracy. Emperor Shah Jehan, builder of the Taj Mahal, would stage outdoor all-white banquets under the full moon, with white carpets on the terrace, white-clad guests seated on white cushions amid arrangements of scented white flowers, and an all-white menu including dishes like *safed murgh korma,* in which skinned chicken breasts are cooked in a sauce of ground blanched almonds, yogurt, and sweet spices.

Northern India is heavily Muslim, so chicken and lamb are popular. Biryanis are cousins to Middle Eastern pilafs, while tandoori chicken, which is unique to India, is justly popular in restaurants throughout the West, and tandoori prawns are, in my opinion, even better.

South Indian food is primarily Hindi and therefore vegetarian, except for the Christian communities in Goa and elsewhere. It is also the area of India most affected by the innovations brought by the spice trade and by the food traditions of neighboring Indonesia. Rice is the staple; dal, yogurt, and cheese are the proteins; and an array of vegetables with highly spiced sauces give interest to these basic flavors. For meat eaters, vindaloo style involves marinating goat, lamb, chicken, or shrimp in a mixture of vinegar, pepper, and spices—

including lots of garlic—before slow cooking and serving with more chiles. It's a technique from Goa, the formerly Portuguese area where chiles first reached India and vinegar (not a native Indian ingredient) was familiar. Andhra Pradesh, on the Bay of Bengal, has the hottest, spiciest dishes in India— heavy on the garlic and cardamom as well as the chiles.

The cuisines of the north rely on a variety of savory skillet breads for carbohydrates, and they tend to use thick sauces that can cling to a *naan* or a chapati without making it soggy. The rice-based cooking of the south uses thinner sauces that soak into the grains in what author Kenneth Lo, in another context, calls "a savory lava."

 NEPAL/TIBET These cuisines combine some traditions of neighboring India and China with the exigencies of an extreme climate. Rice is often replaced by barley, buckwheat, or potatoes. Tsampa—toasted barley flour—is eaten alone, mixed into broths or mixed with buttered tea, a staple that provides needed moisture and fat in the harsh climate. Tibetan food writer Rinjing Dorje says a Tibetan may commonly drink forty cups of tea a day (small cups, I should add). The combination of a Buddhist vegetarian ethos and the realities of nomadic life in the highlands makes for a series of compromises. Tibetan Buddhists eat dairy products, especially yak milk, yogurt, and butter, when they can, and meat when they must. As all lives are held to be of equal value, when they do have to eat an animal killed for meat, they prefer to choose a large one.

North Africa/Middle East/Mediterranean

Thousands of years as a crossroads of trade and conquest has left this region with some of the world's most sophisticated cuisines. Although Provençal and North African cooking has become increasingly popular, the food of Iraq, Saudi Arabia, and other Arabic countries has been largely unknown. A primarily Muslim population means heavy reliance on lamb and seafood and little use of pork. The food images of the Koran are full of fruit and sweets, and these tastes continue into modern cooking, which combines fruit inventively with meat, and serves it on its own in subtly flavored compotes and salads.

Modern Arabic cooking still shows the traces of past meetings of a nomadic culture, whose hospitality was as legendary as its resources were scarce, with a sophisticated, pleasure-seeking urban population who lived at a center for trade and innovations. In medieval Baghdad, nomadic Arabs who lived on dates, barley, mutton, and *kishk,* were introduced to grains, fruits, and seasonings from all around the Mediterranean and beyond— raisins and olives, chickpeas and fava beans from the farmlands of Egypt. They bought sesame seeds to grind into tahini to mix with their yogurt and yogurt cheeses, apples from the Syrian highlands, millet and rice, fresh fish and pigeons, spices and vegetables from India and Persia, and essences of rose and orange blossom and jasmine to add their perfume to the sensual blend of spices. The arrival of chiles and tomatoes from the New World brought another level of diversity to Middle Eastern cooking, with some cultures diving with enthusiasm into fiery foods, making harissa sauces and other condiments, and others concentrating on bright combinations of tomato or cucumber with fresh herbs and lemon juice. The combination of austerity and sensuality in food reaches its climax during the religious observance of Ramadan, the month when Muslims fast from sunrise to sunset, all the while building their anticipation for a night of feasting.

Arabic food preparation tends to be time-consuming in the extreme, involving simple ingredients that are transformed by many steps and requiring a tableful of separate dishes to truly meet the standards of generosity. If you have ever wondered what all those traditional Arab women do when confined to their homes, try a classic couscous with seven vegetables, or a *meze* spread, and wonder no more. The relevant Arabic saying is "The woman killed herself with work, yet the feast lasted only one day." Still, with a food processor and a slightly less ambitious definition of hospitality, Arab food is well within the reach of the North American table and well worth the trouble.

The best-known feature of the Arab kitchen is *meze,* an array of small appetizers—salads, pickles, dips (such as hummus and baba ganoosh), meat tarts, spinach and cheese pastries, sliced tomatoes with mint and feta, olives, and a selection of fragrant spiced breads. Sauces are often similar to Mexican salsas, with chunky tomatoes, chiles, cilantro, lemon, and olive oil.

Yogurt and yogurt cheese, both popular throughout the Middle East, are part of the nomadic tradition, which has no storage for fresh milk and not enough time in one spot to make hard cheeses. Wheat is another staple, usually the hard durum variety that can be harvested before the weather gets too hot. Syria has exported wheat since the days of the Roman Empire. Couscous, which requires drying wheat in the sun, is a practical food in the North African climate. In Yemen, a loaf of whole-wheat bread is the foundation of most meals, while in North Africa, fiery harissa and a little lamb, chicken, or fish flavor a large mound of couscous. In the Arabian Gulf states *kebsa,* a paella-like rice dish, and delicate basmati pilafs crowned with seafood and rich with spices conceal a treasure of healthy vegetables.

The emphasis on mutton in Middle Eastern cooking has had several salutary effects. Meatballs, *koftas,* and other minced dishes make the most of tough nomadic livestock and the slow cooking methods favored in the region. Sweet and sour flavors and tangy fruit sauces pair well with the strongly flavored mutton. The overall flavoring ranges from predominantly sweet, as in Morocco and Iran, to blazing hot, as in Morocco and Tunisia.

Moroccan cuisine in particular reflects the influence of the Spanish Jews as well as itinerant spice traders, Roman administrators, and Berber nomads from the Sahara. It is most characterized by the daring and successful combinations of a bit of meat with sweet spices, dried fruits, and nuts.

Fruit, raisins, and pine nuts appear frequently in main dishes as well as desserts. Perfumed rice puddings and syrupy multi-layered pastries filled with nuts are favorites in every Arab nation, washed down with strong sweet tea or coffee.

Part Two

————————— ❧ —————————

Alphabetical Listing

Many ingredients and preparations have several common names. Check the index for a cross-reference if you do not find what you are looking for.

❧ A ❧

Abon (Indonesian, Chinese) Fried, sweetened spiced flakes of poultry, beef, pork, or seafood, popular as a garnish for rice or other plain dishes. It is sold packaged in Asian markets.

Abura agé (Japanese) Thin, deep-fried tofu, available plain and fresh, refrigerated, or frozen, as well as canned with seasoning (called *inari zushi no moto*), in Japanese markets. Rinse off some of the excess oil with hot water before using. It should be eaten within three days after thawing; don't refreeze it. This can be added in strips to stir fries, or used as a wrapping for meats and vegetables, then simmered in broth.

Acar, atjar (Indonesian) Spiced cooked vegetables, often cabbage, with vinegar and chiles. Available in jars in some supermarkets and Asian markets.

Achiote condimentado (Latin American) A powdery block of annatto, garlic, vinegar (or orange juice or water), and spices, one of the many *recados* that ground Yucatecan cooking. You crumble a bit into your sauce or broth for color and flavor. This is great with chicken. See also **Annatto** and **Recado**.

RECIPE REFERENCE: **Pollo in Escabeche Rojo,** *The Art of Mexican Cooking,* p. 430.

Ackee, akee (Caribbean, African) The fruit of a West African tree (*Blighia sapida*), ackee was introduced to Jamaica by Captain Bligh in 1793, after playing an important supporting role in the mutiny on the *Bounty*. Ackee are more or less pear-shaped with a scarlet shell. When ripe they split open, revealing the black shiny seeds and creamy colored lobed innards, sometimes known for their looks as *vegetable brains*. The texture when cooked is somewhat like sweetbreads, soft and tender but not mushy, and the taste is bland but satisfying, a good foil for salty and spicy flavors. West Africans eat them raw, which some books say is dangerous because they are toxic if either overripe or underripe. What definitely is true is that that they spoil very quickly once they have been cleaned and washed. To prepare fresh ackee you must first remove the seeds and any black or reddish specks on the fleshy lobes. If you are not going to use them immediately, either freeze them or coat with cooking oil, unrefrigerated and unwashed. Moisture is the enemy of ripe ackee; they spoil very quickly if damp. Ackee are available canned in Caribbean markets. The Jamaican national dish, salt fish and ackee, is absolutely delicious. See also **Salt fish**.

RECIPE: Salt Fish and Ackee
From Ethlyn Hilton of Falmouth, Jamaica.

> $^1/_2$ pound salt cod
> 2 dozen fresh or 1 can ackee
> $^1/_2$ cup cooking oil
> 1 large onion, chopped
> 4 scallions, chopped
> 2 tomatoes, chopped
> salt and pepper to taste

Soak cod overnight. Drain and boil with cleaned ackee until the ackee is tender. Remove fish; drain ackee. Separate and bone the fish flakes. In a skillet, heat oil and add onion and scallions and cook until soft. Add tomatoes and cook through. Add ackee and fish, heat together, and serve. Often served with fried breadfruit. Serves 4.

Agar-agar, kanten, tai choy (Chinese, Japanese) A processed seaweed that is most familiar as a jelling agent but can also be used in salad. It comes dried in sheets, rectangular blocks, or flakes, colored white or red. Use the sheets and strips for cooking, soaking them first to reconstitute. To use as gelatin, soak flakes in hot water until they dissolve and then strain out any lumps.

To use in salads, soak 2 hours in cold water, changing water once or twice, and then cut into 2-inch lengths and tear these into shreds. Dried agar keeps indefinitely without refrigeration. It makes a firmer gelatin than the meat-based American aspics and does not require refrigeration, but unflavored gelatin can be substituted in a pinch.

Agé (Japanese) Deep-fried tofu pouches sold in Japanese markets, ready to stuff with vegetables, grains, fruit, and so on. Then they can be eaten as is like a pita sandwich, or refried.

Agresto, verjus (European) Juice of unripe grapes, used in some Italian and French recipes instead of vinegar.

Ají colór (South American) Mild, dried pepper powder, similar to and interchangeable with sweet paprika. It is popular in Chile and Argentina, which have large European populations and are not so inclined to fiery hot foods. *Ají* is a generic South American term for "chile."

Ajowan, bishop's-weed, omam, ajwain, carom (Indian, Ethiopian, Middle Eastern) Seed of the ancient European herb *lovage*. The plants are related to caraway and cumin, and the seeds show that family resemblance. The taste is variously described as sharp, piquant, and bitter, but it is not so strong that it doesn't show up in cookies and pastries. It is a common ingredient in Ethiopian *berbere* sauce and is used in Indian breads such as *naan, pakora,* and *paratha;* in vegetable pickles; and as an ingredient in *chat masala.* It's sold whole in Indian and Arabic markets.

Aleppo pepper, filful ahmar halaby (Middle Eastern) A red pepper, coarsely ground without seeds. It is valued for its fragrance and flavor, which complement the sweet spicing of Arabic food, in addition to its heat. It's expensive and not always easy to find. Seeded guajillo peppers are a good substitute and serranos a reasonable one.

Amaranth, Chinese spinach, tampala, alegria bledo, hiyu, chaulai (Chinese, Mexican, Caribbean, Latin American) As the range of common names indicates, this ancient plant is widespread. Both the greens and the tiny seeds are used. The fresh greens are most commonly found in Asian markets, although they may also show up in Caribbean groceries labeled "callaloo." They differ, however, from the taro leaves which also are used to make the islands' famous callaloo soup. Confusing, no? The young greens taste similar to spinach, though a bit stronger. As the plants get older, the leaves develop a rather metallic taste that can overpower other ingredients. Canned amaranth, pickled in salt, is also sold in most Asian markets. The seeds and flour may be found in Latin American markets and in natural foods stores, where it has been going through a recent period of trendiness.

Amchoor (Indian) Dried, powdered green mango, sold in bulk in Indian stores. It is used as a souring agent for dals and fried vegetables (*chaat*). One Indian technique is to stuff okra with a bit of *amchoor* and *garam masala,* and then braise it with tomato, eggplant, and ginger. I have used *amchoor* to simulate green mango, using apple slices instead of mango. Sprinkle them with salt and let them sit for 20 minutes to make them more pliable. Rinse off the salt, sprinkle with *amchoor,* and use in place of mango.

Amradeen (Middle Eastern) Thin sheets of sun-dried puréed apricots, sometimes mixed with sugar and olive oil. The sheets are a beautiful glistening rich orange. I have found them in Arabic markets, imported from Syria. *Amradeen* is used for its flavor and soft texture as part of the many sweet and sour sauces of Arabic cuisine. The recipe given here is from Iraq.

RECIPE REFERENCE: **Grilled Eggplant with Apricot Pomegranate Sauce (Beitinjan bil Hamod)**, *The Arabian Delights Cookbook,* p. 132.

Anaheim chile Long, green, and mild, this chile is used for *chiles rellenos* and in salsas. It is also available ripe (red), dried, and powdered. The Anaheim chile is one of the most common fresh chiles in North American markets.

Ancho chile (Mexican, Latin American) A dried version of *chile poblano, ancho chiles* are sold in Mexican markets and many supermarkets. The peppers are wide at the top, heart-shaped, and usually dark red to brown or black when dried. (Fresh *poblanos* are green and are standard for *chiles rellenos*.) They are much used in moles, and their mild flavor and sweet, pungent odor complements the ground seeds and hotter spices. One batch I bought in Mexico had an overly bitter edge that detracted from the dish; I found that by soaking them for 10 minutes in warm water and discarding the water, I could get the taste back in balance.

Annatto, achuete, atsuete, bifol, roucou, hot dieu (Latin American, Pan-Asian, Indian) Brick-red seeds, used more for color than for flavor, which is just a bit astringent and slightly "dusty." They are sometimes sold as a cheap, but not satisfactory, substitute for saffron. The seeds are soaked in water or cooked in oil to bring out the color, and then discarded. You also can buy liquid annatto extract. See also **Achiote condimentado**.

Ao nori (Japanese) Dried green seaweed sold in a sprinkle bottle and used as a garnish for soup and rice.

Arborio rice (Italian) The best-known of the many types of medium-grained, highly polished rices used to make risottos and paella. To make risotto, *arborio* rice is coated first in a *soffritto* of olive oil, herbs, and wine, and then cooked with the gradual addition of simmering stock. The resulting grain, served *al dente* in a creamy sheen of rice starch and rich flavors, is as delicious as and about as different as possible from the fluffiest and most tender basmati pilaf.

Arepas (Latin American) The cornbread of Venezuela and Colombia, made like tortillas from a masa rather than from straight ground cornmeal, but differing in cooking technique and in the type of corn used. Look for *harina por arepas* in Latin markets before trying an *arepa* recipe with regular masa. *Arepas* are thicker than tortillas and may be first grilled and then baked, giving them a crisp outside and a softer interior. *Arepas de chocolo* are made with fresh corn kernals, ground, kneaded, and roasted. You can approximate traditional arepas by stirring a cup of boiling water into an equal amount of cooked white cornmeal. Add a bit of butter and salt, pat into tortillas, and grill.

Asafetida, hing, perunkaya (Indian, Pan-Asian) Resin from the plant *Ferula assafoetida,* used in tiny quantities as a flavoring and an antiflatulent in curries. Once cooked, asafetida has an mild, oniony taste that is preferred in India by groups such as the Jains and some Brahmins, who are forbidden strong-tasting food and therefore avoid real onions. Asafetida was popular in classical Greece and Rome, although it is rarely used in Europe today. Nowadays it is sold in Indian markets, often in a small can cryptically labeled "brown *khada*," as amber-colored chunks of resin or ground into a pale yellow powder. If you buy the resin, you have to grind it before use, but the payoff is that the aroma is not released until it's ground. (Its common names, *devil's dung* and *stinking gum,* should be a clue as to its potency.) If you have the powder, lock it up tight lest the smell take over your kitchen. A related type, *Ferula narthex,* is not as strong. Its leaves and stems are sold as a vegetable in markets in Afghanistan and Iran. See also **Chat masala.**

RECIPE REFERENCE: Sesame-Tamarind Chutney Powder, *Flatbreads and Flavors,* pp. 167–168.

Asfor (Middle Eastern) Stamens of the safflower, used to color rice and to flavor Levantine (Eastern Mediterranean) dishes. They are a pretty light orange and are sometimes passed off as saffron for a too-good-to-be-true price.

RECIPE REFERENCE: Saudi Fish Soup, *The Arabian Delights Cookbook,* p. 103.

Asian pears, pae (Japanese, Korean) Large, round, crisp, and delicately flavored, these have more the texture of an apple, but with a milder taste. They have nothing of the buttery smoothness of a European dessert pear. Imported ones often are tasteless, the result of premature picking. Domestic ones are available in some groceries and farmers' markets and are a much better choice.

Asparagus bean, Chinese bean, yard-long bean, sitao, kacang panjang (Chinese, Thai, Indonesian) A different genus (*Vigna* rather than *Phaseolus*), from more familiar string beans, these beans can actually grow a yard long. They have a mild flavor and a firmer, crunchier texture than regular green beans. They are commonly sold in Asian markets, where they are coiled up like little lassos. Look for the brighter, flatter ones when you shop.

RECIPE REFERENCE: **Karedok,** *Indonesian Regional Cooking,* pp. 160–161. *A vegetable salad from West Java.*

Ate, guava paste (Latin American, European, North African, Middle Eastern) A sweetened fruit paste, usually of guava or quince, common in Mexico, Cuba (where it is used as a cake frosting), and other Latin countries via Moorish Spain and the Middle East, where it makes Turkish delight. *Ates* keep a long time and can be served alone as a dessert or with cheese, a fortuitous combination that contrasts the smooth texture and full flavor of the cheese with the somewhat bland sweetness and grainy texture of the *ate*.

Atsuagé (Japanese) Tofu cutlets, pressed free of water and then deep-fried, steamed, or baked. They are sometimes marinated first. The name means "thick; fry."

Atta flour (Indian) Hard whole-wheat flour, very finely ground, sold in some Indian and South Asian groceries and used for chapatis, *naan*, and other flatbreads. If you can't find it, natural foods stores often sell fine-ground whole-wheat flour. Or you can take regular whole-wheat bread flour and sift out most of the bran.

RECIPE: **Savory Country Corn Bread (Tikkar)**
Flatbreads and Flavors, pp. 136–137. *From Rajasthan, India.*

2 1/2 cups atta or whole-wheat flour
1 cup corn flour
1/4 teaspoon salt
1 small onion, chopped
1 1-inch piece fresh ginger, peeled and chopped fine
2 large garlic cloves, chopped fine
1 jalapeño, seeded and chopped fine
1 medium tomato, chopped fine
2–3 tablespoons fresh coriander leaves
1 1/2 cups lukewarm water
6–8 tablespoons vegetable oil or ghee

Combine flours and salt in a bowl and mix will. Add onion, ginger, garlic, jalapeño, tomato, and coriander, and mix well. Make a well in the center and pour in 1 1/2 cups water, stirring it into the flour. Add more water if needed to make a kneadable dough; more flour if it's too goopy. Knead 4–5 minutes on a lightly floured surface.

Wash, dry, and lightly oil the bowl. Return dough to bowl, cover, and rest 30 minutes. Divide dough into 8 pieces. Flatten each piece on a floured surface, flouring both sides. Cover the 8 discs with plastic wrap (don't stack them) and set aside. Roll out discs into circles approximately 7 inches in diameter by $1/4$ inch thick.

To cook, heat one or two heavy skillets over medium heat. Transfer a rolled-out circle to a skillet. Cook 7 minutes or until the bottom is covered with brown speckles. Turn and cook on the other side for approximately the same length of time. Brush about a teaspoon of oil or ghee on top of the bread, turn over, and fry 1 minute until golden brown. Brush second side with oil or ghee, flip the bread, and fry for 1 more minute. Transfer to a plate and serve as soon as possible. Makes 8 seven-inch rounds.

Avocado leaf (Latin American) Avocados are members of the laurel family, the same tree that produces bay leaves, and their large, tapered leaves are used the same way in some Mexican recipes—Oaxacan *barbacoas,* for example. Toast them on an ungreased skillet or griddle for about a minute on each side. You can have a constant supply at home by planting an avocado pit in a pot by a sunny window. In fact, you can have a six-foot indoor tree within a year or two. However, Mexican food doyenne Diana Kennedy warns that the indoor plants have very little flavor.

RECIPE REFERENCE: Tamales de Pescado, *The Art of Mexican Cooking,* p. 82.

Azuki bean (Pan-Asian) A small red bean sold in Asian markets. Its slightly sweet flavor is often augmented with sugar and used in red bean paste, which is stuffed in steamed buns and used in jellies and puddings. You can buy the paste canned. Leftover bean paste will keep for months refrigerated.

❧ B ❧

Babáco (South American) A hybrid papaya, occurring naturally in the lowlands of Ecuador and now being grown commercially. *Babácos* are five-sided, with edible golden skin, white fragrant flesh, and a flavor described as a cross between a pineapple and a banana. This fruit is sometimes found in specialty markets and definitely worth a try. Probably it won't be fully ripe when you buy it; give it a few days to soften at room temperature, and then eat it raw, alone or in a fruit salad.

Bagoong guisado (Philippine) A prepared sauce of shrimp paste, fried with a sweet-and-sour mixture of garlic, onion, tomato, vinegar, and sugar. Foods cooked with shrimp paste are referred to generically as *binagoongan,* and *guisado* means "sautéed."

Bamboo leaves (Asian) Dried bamboo leaves from subtropical China are used to wrap food, imparting a subtle flavor. They are sold in bundles in Asian groceries.

Bamboo shoots, labong (Chinese, Philippine, Southeast Asian) Canned shoots are familiar, and sometimes you also can find them already cooked in soy sauce, but Asian markets may sell fresh ones, as whole, spike-shaped roots in water. Sales are seasonal; winter shoots are more tender, and spring shoots are bigger. Fresh ones are expensive, and good quality canned shoots (look for those labeled "winter," or else "tips") are preferable to tired fresh ones. If you do find good fresh shoots, they should be boiled at least 5 minutes prior to use to get rid of the bitter taste (and the hydrocyanic acid that causes it). Discard the water and with it the unappetizing smell of the fresh sprouts. They will keep in water several days in the refrigerator, with the water changed daily.

RECIPE REFERENCE: **Bok Choy Stir-Fried with Bamboo Shoots and Mushrooms,** *From the Earth: Chinese Vegetarian Cooking,* pp. 76–77.

Banana (Pan-Asian, Caribbean, Latin American) Nearly all bananas sold in U.S. supermarkets are the same variety, Gros Michel. Where bananas actually grow, the variety is bewildering. Sometimes local favorites show up in ethnic markets or well-stocked supermarkets. Thai desserts commonly feature egg and apple bananas. Vietnamese *chuoi nuong,* in which a banana is coated with a sticky mass of sweetened rice mixed with coconut, then wrapped in a banana leaf and grilled, uses tiny finger bananas, whose dry texture helps the rice adhere. (These would also be a good choice for the chocolate-covered frozen bananas my children love to make.) See also **Plantains.**

Banana flower, jantung pisang (Philippine, Indonesian, Southeast Asian) The large, purple, fleshy flower of the banana tree, which is (I bet you didn't know this) an annual. The flowers sometimes show up fresh or dried in Asian markets. They are cooked as a vegetable, as in the slow-cooked Philippine pork hock dish *paksiw na pata,* or marinated lightly in a sugar-and-vinegar dressing and used in salads, such as Vietnamese *goi bap chuoi.*

Banana leaves (Pan-Asian, Latin American) These are huge leaves when whole, as much as two by ten feet. They are more usually found frozen, or sometimes cured for storage, in Asian and Latin markets. With the tough center rib cut out, they are used to wrap fish and poultry (and tamales in some parts of Mexico) for baking or steaming. Their delicate flavor is absorbed by the ingredients they enclose.

Banh trang (Vietnamese, Chinese) Translucent, dried, round or fan-shaped rice-paper wrappers used to make spring rolls and to wrap cooked meats. They are usually sold in stacks and must be carefully loosened all the way around before you can separate them without tearing. To moisten a wrapper, place it in luke-warm water for about 30 seconds, drain on a towel, and then use immediately. If you want a crisper texture, use sugar water or beer. You might be able to find fresh ones, *banh uot,* in Vietnamese communities.

Baobab, kuka, monkey bread (African) My most indelible associations of the baobab tree are menacing images of them taking over a tiny planet in *The Little Prince.* It turns out that the baobab is a true staff of life; nearly every part supplies nourishment. It has large, teardrop-shaped fruits with a flavor somewhat like grapefruit, but a drier texture. The leaves are added to stews as a potherb or, more commonly, dried and powdered and sold as a thickener, like gumbo filé or okra, giving the slippery texture prized in African cooking. The seeds, called *monkey* *bread,* are steeped for a sweet drink, roasted and eaten, or made into *lalu* powder, which acts as a mild baking powder. Even the ash from the burned wood is used to make a saltlike flavoring.

Barfi (Indian) Fudgelike confections sold in Indian delicatessens. These unfortunately named treats are made of slow-cooked groundnuts, coconut, or flavored milk, reduced until they solidify into a soft, grainy-textured mass. They are delicately flavored with rosewater, *kewra,* and other essences and often decorated with sheets of edible silver *varak.* See also **Varak.**

Basmati rice (Indian) A long-grained, fragile, wonderfully fragrant rice, grown at the base of the Himalayas, that is the foundation of the elegant Moghul pilafs and biryanis. It is now sold in most supermarkets, but if you have an Indian or Arabic market nearby you can get it for much less. I buy it at the local Sikh-owned gas station for sixty cents a pound. In order to give basmati its due, you should soak it in cold water for 30 minutes before cooking, and then cook it about 25 minutes in the resulting milky liquid.

Bean threads, glass noodles, cellophane noodles, silver noodles, Chinese vermicelli, long rice, sotanghon (Chinese, Philippine, Japanese, Pan-Asian) Noodles made from mung bean starch, folded into skeins about six inches long and packaged in plastic or net bags. They can be soaked, rather than cooked, about 30 seconds in hot water, but they also can be simmered without dissolving. It is this capacity to absorb liquid and flavor without falling apart or getting mushy that earns them the name "solid gravy," from Chinese food authority Kenneth Lo. Use them in stir fries, soups, and salads, or rinse with cold water and drain, flavor to taste, and add meat and vegetables. When cooked or soaked in water they have a slippery texture and a glassy look. When deep-fried without presoaking they expand dramatically, becoming opaque and brittle. Then they are used as a crisp base for salads.

Beehoon, bihun (Southeast Asian) A thin rice vermicelli used in curried dishes, stir fries, and soups.

Berbere (East African) A hot chile powder, sometimes sold as a paste, much used in Ethiopian and other East African cooking. It's essential to the proper flavor of the famous Ethiopian chicken stew *doro wat*. Chile is the main ingredient, but the taste is smoothed and sweetened by the addition of sweet spices such as cinnamon and cardamom, and ajowan, onions, and garlic.

Bharaat (Middle Eastern) A sweet spice mixture from the Levant, using, in one version, allspice, cinnamon, nutmeg, and cloves. It is used in rice dishes.

Bird's nest (Chinese) Not a poetic name but the real thing, made of the gelatinous substance produced by the cliff swallows of the South China Sea when they regurgitate marine food for their young. It is expensive, it's a sign of honor to serve it to an important guest, and it's supposed to be good for your skin, but it doesn't have a whole lot of taste. Bird's nests are sold dried. Whole, cleaned nests are the most expensive; next come broken chips called *dragon's teeth*; ground-up fragments are the cheapest and most common. After soaking them overnight in cold water, simmer 20 minutes in plain water, rinse in cold water, and squeeze dry. Add the resulting jellylike strands to soups and sauces.

Bitter leaf (West African) Smallish, dark leaves, sold dried in African markets; used in stews and side dishes including the most famous of all African sauces, palaver sauce, which uses bitter leaf with tripe, fish, salt pork, beef, and sometimes chicken. When African slaves came to the Americas they substituted wild greens and strong flavored potherbs such as collards and mustard greens for their bitter leaf, and so can you. Kale may be the closest in flavor of the commonly available North American vegetables.

Bitter melon, karela, ampalaya, balsam pear (Chinese, Indian, Philippine) An oblong fruit up to a foot in length and two to three inches across. The payoff to its bitter edge, which comes from quinine, is a bright, refreshing aftertaste that makes it popular as a summer vegetable. Available fresh in Asian and Indian markets (where it will be labeled "karela"), it has shiny green-to-yellowish bumpy skin and a spongy or hollow center with a lot of seeds. The more yellow in the color, the milder the melon. It is also sold canned and dried. Chinese cooks use bitter melon in stir fries with meats or seafood. They also steam it, stuff it with pork or shrimp, and add it to soups. In India it may also be blanched, stuffed with a spicy vegetable mixture, and sautéed—a lot of work but a wonderful dish.

Biznaga, acitrón, candied cactus (Latin American) Candied cactus (*Echniocactus grandis*). Bland and very sweet in the Mexican dulce style and not exciting served on its own. Sometimes used in *picadillos,* meat stuffings, and sweet tamales.

Black glutinous rice, pulut hitam, hak loh mai, karuppu poolor A long-grained, dark-colored rice resembling North American wild rice, though very different in flavor and texture. It is most used in sweet dishes from Indonesia and the Philippines, both as flour and cooked with coconut milk and sugar.

Blood orange (European, North African) A small orange with spooky, deep red flesh. It has long been popular in Spain and is available in some U.S. specialty markets. The flavor is intense, like a really good Valencia. This is an ancient Middle Eastern variety, brought to Spain by the Moslems in the Middle Ages.

Bomba rice (Spanish) A Mediterranean variety, used for paella, that is creamy textured and nearly round.

Breadfruit (Pan-Asian, Latin American, Caribbean, African) A native fruit of southern Asian and Pacific islands. Bland and starchy, it was imported to the Caribbean as a cheap food for slaves and from there traveled on slave ships to Africa. The fresh fruit is green, about ten inches around, with a warty skin. It looks like a small alligator-skin bowling ball. It is treated much like a potato—fried in slices, plain boiled, or cubed, boiled, and mashed. On some Caribbean islands, such as Grenada, it is used in place of potatoes to make vichyssoise. The Jamaican pattern is to roast the fruit over a wood fire or gas flame, scrape off the charred skin, and then fry. This gives a wonderful smoky contrast to the bland interior. It's often served with salt fish and ackee and is used in breads, pies, and puddings. Canned breadfruit is sold in almost any Asian or Latin American market. Fresh and frozen breadfruit may also be available.

———————— ᴥ§ ————————

RECIPE: **Breadfruit with Tomato Sauce**
A West African Cookbook, p. 150.

> One 16-ounce can breadfruit chunks
> 4 tablespoons peanut or other light vegetable oil
> 1 large onion, peeled and thinly sliced
> 3 or 4 tomatoes, peeled and thinly sliced
> 1–2 tablespoons tomato paste
> $1/3$ cup breadfruit liquid from can
> 1 teaspoon ground red pepper or to taste
> 1 teaspoon salt
> parsley and chives

Drain breadfruit, saving liquid. Heat oil in a frying pan. Fry onion until soft, add tomatoes, and cook until thick and well blended. Add tomato paste, breadfruit liquid, and seasonings. Mix well and cook 5–10 minutes. Arrange breadfruit pieces on top of sauce, turning to coat each piece. Heat through. Sprinkle with parsley and chives before serving. Serves 6.

————————— ✁ —————————

Brem (Balinese) Rice wine.

Briouats (North African, Middle Eastern) Filled pastry triangles from Morocco. Traditionally they are made with *warka* pastry, but they can be done with *filo*. One filling is blanched almonds, cinnamon, sugar, orange blossom water, and butter, another is date and almond, and yet another is ground beef with harissa and spices. See also **Harissa** and **warka**.

Buckwheat (Eastern European, Asian) Kasha is probably the best-known food made from this hardy seed. It makes a light-textured, almost crunchy pilaf with a nutty taste. Buckwheat flour is used to make noodles in Korea and Japan, and the flour is used for skillet breads from Finland to North Africa to Tibet. One of the few grains that can be grown in the short seasons and extreme conditions of the Himalayas, its flour is roasted and mixed with water or tea to make the ubiquitous Tibetan food tsampa. So basic is this food to Tibetan life that pinches of tsampa are passed out to guests at Tibetan New Year's celebrations to ensure food for the coming year.

Burdock, gobo, uong (Japanese, Korean) The long, brownish, hairy root of the infamous cocklebur plant, whose seeds were the inspiration for Velcro. Gobo is sold fresh, dried, and canned in Asian markets, and is an ingredient in many Asian herbal remedies and tonics as a promoter of strength and endurance, sexual and otherwise. Japanese delis often feature gobo/carrot tempura and other gobo mixtures as a snack food, and in Korea it makes a famous kimchee, a hallmark of Kyongsang Province. Burdock has a delicious, earthy flavor—not as sweet as a carrot, richer than a potato. When you buy it fresh, a good root will be breakable, not limp, but don't expect it to be as crisp as a carrot. Store it refrigerated and use within a few days. Dried and shaved gobo is added to stews, vegetables, and bean or grain dishes. Canned gobo should be avoided unless you're desperate, and it's a little hard to imagine being that desperate for burdock.

RECIPE: **Kimpira Gobo**
Winter Harvest, p. 183.

1 1/2 pounds gobo
2 tablespoons oil, divided
1/3 to 1/2 cup tamari
2 teaspoons sugar
1/4 cup dried shrimp
1/2-inch piece fresh chile pepper, chopped, or
      1/4 teaspoon dried red pepper flakes

Scrub gobo, peel, and slice into 2-inch matchsticks. Soak for 20 minutes in cold water. Mix 1 tablespoon of the oil, tamari, and sugar in a small bowl. Heat the remaining tablespoon of oil in a medium skillet, add shrimp, and sauté briefly over medium-high heat. Drain gobo, add to skillet, and cook 2 or 3 minutes. Add tamari mixture and cook, stirring often, until most of the liquid is absorbed. Gobo should still be crisp. Add chile pepper or pepper flakes and serve. Serves 4.

Bzar (North African) The Libyan take on masala, a mixture of sweet and hot spices in several combinations. One version is 1 tablespoon cinnamon, 1 1/2 teaspoons red pepper, 1 teaspoon nutmeg, 1 teaspoon cloves, 1 teaspoon turmeric, 1 teaspoon ground ginger, 1 teaspoon allspice, 1 teaspoon black pepper, and 2 teaspoons cumin (optional). It's used to flavor rice, potatoes, and other vegetable dishes.

RECIPE REFERENCE: **New Potatoes with Bzar (Batatis bi Bzar)**, *The Arabian Delights Cookbook,* p. 146.

❧ C ☙

Calabaza, calabash, ahuyama, zapallo, abobora, West Indian pumpkin, green pumpkin (Latin American) **Calabaza** is the most generic term for the large winter squashes common in Latin America and the Caribbean. Despite the English names, these are not pumpkins and have the sweeter flavor and harder flesh of a Hubbard or sweetmeat squash, both of which make good substitutes.

Callaloo, bhaji (Caribbean, Indian) Actually two plants, used interchangeably in the most famous eponymous Caribbean soup. One is the taro leaf and the other is Chinese spinach, also known as amaranth. Whichever plant they come from, the leaves are thinner and more richly flavored than spinach, and they add the perfect note to the mildness of coconut milk and fresh seafood. See also **Amaranth, Taro.**

────────── ❧ ──────────

RECIPE: **Callaloo**

The Cooking of the Caribbean Islands, by Linda Wolfe, p. 45. *A crab and greens soup from Barbados.*

$^1/_2$ pound callaloo greens, spinach, or chard

3 tablespoons butter

$^1/_2$ cup onion, finely chopped

^{1}/$_2$ teaspoon garlic, finely chopped
3 cups chicken stock
^{1}/$_2$ cup coconut milk
1 teaspoon salt
freshly ground black pepper
^{1}/$_2$ pound crab meat, fresh, canned, or frozen
dash A-1 or Pickapeppa sauce

Wash greens. Leave the thinner callaloo greens whole, but shred spinach or chard. Melt butter in a heavy casserole. Add onion and garlic and cook 5 minutes, stirring frequently, until they are transparent but not brown. Add greens and turn with a spoon for 4 or 5 minutes, until they soften.

Stir in chicken stock, coconut milk, salt, and pepper. Bring to a boil over high heat, reduce to low, and simmer uncovered for about 10 minutes or until greens are tender. Add crab meat and hot sauce and heat through, stirring. Taste for seasoning and serve at once. Serves 4–6.

Calpis (Japanese) A sweet syrup, usually white, used to make a popular Japanese soft drink. Sometimes also available in orange and grape. Sold in Japanese stores like syrups for Italian sodas and coffee drinks. Dilute to taste and serve over ice. *Calpis* drinks are also sold canned as soda pop, and are an inexpensive way to try out the flavor. (Japanese markets also stock dizzying varieties of canned sweetened teas and coffees.)

Camotes (Latin American) Indigenous Mexican sweet potatoes. Mexican cooking expert Diana Kennedy says to bake them in the evening, pack them in a casserole where they begin to sweat out their sweet syrup, and serve the next morning for breakfast.

Candlenuts, kemiri, buah keras (Indonesian, Malaysian, Thai) The fruit of the candleberry tree, *Aleurites moluccana,* these tough-shelled nuts are ground and used as a thickener and binder in sauces and curry pastes. You can buy them, shelled and packaged from Indonesia, in some Asian groceries. The cryptic package warning—"This is not a snack"—refers to the slight toxicity of the uncooked nuts. Macadamia nuts are a good substitute.

Cape gooseberry, golden berry, ground cherry, physalis, poha, strawberry tomato (Australian, New Zealand, South African, Indian, Chinese) Like tomatillos, these are relatives of the ornamental Chinese lantern. The fruits are golden yellow and slightly tart, and are good cooked with meat as well as in pies and jams and eaten fresh. Cape gooseberries are picking up speed as a trendy fruit and should soon become more readily available.

Carambola, star fruit, mit, belimbing (Latin American, Caribbean, Vietnamese, Indonesian) The waxy, yellow-green fruit of a tropical evergreen tree. Crosswise slices make a star pattern—hence the name. The watery flesh can be sour or sweet. Most U.S. markets sell the sweet variety, which is rather insipid, and is better for looks than for taste. The favored Asian type is sour, adding piquancy to Vietnamese salads and Indonesian fish dishes. It is also used in Indian pickles and chutneys. The little sour ones are often cooked with Indonesian fish. A tart green apple is a reasonable substitute for sour star fruit.

Cardamom, kapulaga, elaichi (European, Indian, Indonesian, Middle Eastern, North African) The ground dried powder is acceptable for baking, but curries and other dishes benefit from fresh-ground seeds. Cardamom seeds come in several colors. The green ones are my favorite and the most pungent, and are used to flavor Bedouin coffee and Indian tea, as well as hundreds of cooked dishes. The black ones (actually dark brown) are bigger and less intense in flavor, with a nutlike aroma. Many of them in fact come from a different plant.

Cardoon (European, Middle Eastern) A huge thistle that is a botanical cousin to artichoke with a similar flavor, but the blanched stalks are eaten instead of the immature flowers. It is sold fresh at some farmers' markets and European specialty markets. Cardoons need to be blanched before cooking or they are dauntingly bitter. The whiter and firmer the stalks, the more they are worth the effort. A fall and winter crop, they are part of cool-weather meals such as lamb, green olives, and preserved lemon (in Morocco) and *bagna cauda* (in Italy).

RECIPE: **Cardoons Pellegrini**

Winter Harvest Cookbook, p. 169.

> 1 pound cardoons
> 2 ounces lead pork, minced and pounded to a paste
> 2 tablespoons olive oil
> 2 teaspoons butter
> 3 shallots or 1 small onion, minced
> 2 cloves garlic
> 1 tablespoon chopped celery leaves
> $^1/_3$ cup tomato sauce
> $^1/_3$ cup beef or chicken stock
> 3 tablespoons lemon juice

Trim and slice cardoons into 2-inch pieces and blanch 3 or 4 minutes in boiling salted water. Remove and drain. (You can save the cooking water for soup.) Melt salt pork, olive oil, and butter in a skillet. Add shallots or onion, garlic, and celery leaves and sauté gently, watching carefully so mixture does not brown. Add tomato sauce, stock, and lemon juice. Simmer a few minutes until mixture is well blended. Add cardoons, cover, and cook until tender. Serves 4.

Carne seca (Latin American) The Latin American version of beef jerky, sun dried and salted. Available in Latin American markets, or you can substitute a low-fat, non-teriyakied or otherwise fancied-up North American jerky. See also **Gadeed**.

Cascabel chile, chile bola (Latin American) Small and round chiles, red to black in color, not very hot, but flavorful. They are more commonly sold dried, but I have seen fresh ones at the supermarket.

Cashew apple (Caribbean, Central American) The swollen base of the cashew nut, pear-shaped and orange-red when ripe, is a treat in its own right. Sold fresh on some Caribbean islands and in Central America, it is generally stewed or used for jellies or liqueurs. Dried cashew apples are sometimes available in natural foods stores. They somewhat resemble prunes.

Cassareep (Caribbean) Boiled juice from grated cassava root with a bittersweet flavor. Flavored with cinnamon, cloves, and brown sugar, it is used in pepperpot stew. *Cassareep* is sold bottled in West Indian markets, or you can make your own: Peel and grate about 2 pounds of cassava root. Mound half the gratings onto cheesecloth, and squeeze out the juice. Do the same with the other half (you can save the pulp for cassava bread—it freezes well) and pour the juice into a heavy skillet. Cook over medium heat until the juice is smooth and thick, no more than a few minutes.

Cassava, manioc, mandioca, yucca, yuca, singkong, ketéla, ubi kayu (Asian, African, Caribbean, Latin American, Indonesian) The species name, *Manihot utilissima,* is the tip-off to what author Sri Owen describes as this "unexciting but valuable tuber." Cassava has not much taste, but great adaptability as a crop and as a kitchen staple. It is native to South America and the Caribbean but is also popular in Africa and Asia. In North America and Western Europe, it is best known in the forms of tapioca and arrowroot. Raw cassava root contains prussic acid, sometimes in fatal amounts (it was used for suicide by Caribbean Indians who despaired of life under Spanish rule). The acid is removed by long soaking or neutralized by cooking.

Cassava shows up in ethnic markets in several forms. Fresh roots are long, brown, and hairy, about two inches in diameter with hard, white flesh. These can be baked, boiled, or sliced thin and deep-fried into chips. Many markets also sell frozen cooked cassava, either grated or formed into soft balls, ready to use as African *fufu*. Cassava flour and the coarser cassava meal (often sold as manioc) appear in African, Latin American, and Caribbean markets. The Jamaican bread *bammy* is made with cassava flour. Look for *gari* in African markets and *farofa* in Latin American ones. The flour is commonly cooked in palm oil until it makes a golden brown roux, then mixed or boiled with water to make the West African staple *gari fufu*. Toasted cassava, with or without palm oil, is a ubiquitous condiment in Brazil, where it is sprinkled on meat and vegetables rather like Parmesan at a pizza parlor. Cassava leaves are a popular green vegetable, as in Indonesian dishes where they are puréed with dried fish and coconut milk, or cooked with bitter melon. See also **Cassareep**.

———————— 🌿 ————————

RECIPE: **Cassava Biscuits from Barbados**
The Cooking of the Caribbean Islands, by Linda Wolfe, p. 75.

     1 pound sweet cassava
     4 tablespoons butter, softened
     4 tablespoons lard

$^1/_2$ cup sugar
1 egg
1$^1/_2$ cups coconut, finely grated
2 cups flour
1 teaspoon double-acting baking powder

Preheat oven to 400°F. Peel cassava and grate (or thaw frozen grated cassava). Wrap grated root in doubled cheesecloth and squeeze to extract liquid, which can be used for *cassareep.*

Cream butter, lard, and sugar, beating and mashing them against the side of the bowl with a large spoon until the mixture is light and fluffy. Beat in cassava, egg, and coconut. Combine flour and baking powder, and sift onto a sheet of wax paper. Add about $^1/_2$ cup at a time to the creamed mixture, beating well after each addition. Dough should be firm enough to be gathered into a compact ball; add more flour if necessary. When dough becomes too stiff to stir, knead in remaining flour with your hands.

On a lightly floured surface, knead dough for 2 or 3 minutes, pushing it down with the heels of your hands, pressing it forward and folding it back on itself. Then roll into a circle about $^1/_4$ inch thick. Cut into 2-inch rounds. Bake on ungreased sheets in middle of oven for 20 minutes, or until firm and golden. Serve at once. Makes 24 2-inch biscuits.

———————— ☙ ————————

Cassia, Chinese cinnamon, Indian bay leaf, tej passia (Chinese, Indian) An ancient spice related to cinnamon and similar in taste, coming from the bark of an evergreen laurel tree. Cassia is part of the Chinese five-spice mixture. The leaf of the cassia is known as *Indian bay leaf* (*tej patta*) and is longer, thinner, paler, and sweeter flavored than the more familiar North American and European bay laurel. If you substitute bay laurel, use less to allow for its stronger taste.

Cera chile, fresno, chile caribe, wax chile (Latin American) Small, triangular yellow chile with a waxy surface. They are used for pickling or whole in stews, sauces, or lentil dishes. Flavor ranges from mild to a bit hot. (Some books use *fresno* and *Anaheim* interchangeably to describe the longer, green, mildly peppy chiles referred to in this books as *Anaheims*.)

Chaar magaz (Indian) *Chaar* means "four" in Hindi, and *chaar magaz* is a ground mixture of four types of seeds: melon, pumpkin, squash, and watermelon. Cooks around Delhi mix it with a little water and use the paste as a thickening agent and flavoring for curries such as the classic Muslim court dish, white chicken *korma*. Arabic *mahleb,* Mexican *pepian,* and African *egusi* are all ground seed preparations using the same culinary logic.

Chamira (North African) A flour-and-water broth, fermented with vinegar, which is added to Algerian *herira* soup. Sometimes yeast is added also to speed up the process. This tastes much better than it sounds. The soup is truly delicious.

Channa dal, choles, yellow split peas (Indian) A small variety of garbanzos popular in Bengal. They are slow-cooking and sometimes difficult to digest, but the flavor is unbeatable. Cooked whole, they make a wonderful vegetarian curry with potatoes.

They are often cooked with a little asafetida as an antiflatulent, which is useful with these. Puréed and cooked with pomegranate juice, they make the North Indian specialty *chole bhatoore*, served with the deep-fried potato bread *bhatoore* or with *poori*.

RECIPE REFERENCE: **Khatte Channe,** *Classic Indian Cooking,* pp. 272–273.

Cha thai (Thai) Iced tea made of ground tea leaves, vanilla, roasted corn, and orange coloring, put in a cloth bag or coffee filter and brewed several times, then mixed with sugar and milk. Thai households and restaurants used sweetened condensed milk, and so should you if you are trying to duplicate that remembered flavor. The tea is available in bulk in Asian groceries.

Chat masala (Indian) An unusual masala made in one variation with ground asafetida, mint, ginger, ajowan, cayenne, black salt, mango powder, cumin, and dried pomegranate seeds. *Chat* refers to Indian vegetable salads—such as the well-known potato-and-tomato mixture *Chat aloo*—that are seasoned by this mixture.

Chayote, cho-cho, christophine, mirliton, vegetable pear (Latin American, Pan-Asian) A pear-shaped cousin to summer squash, chayote (*Shechium edule*) has a mild flavor somewhat reminiscent of cucumber. Some are green and spiny, others cream colored and light green with ridges rather like an acorn squash. There is one tasty, almond-shaped seed. Chayote is native to Central America but is now widely grown in the subtropics, showing up in markets from Jamaica to Myanmar. It will keep refrigerated up to two weeks. Young ones can be steamed with the peel; older ones have a tough skin and are suitable for stuffing and baking, using the rind as a bowl. Chayote is usually used as a vegetable, but is also sometimes cooked for dessert with sugar and almonds. It's good boiled in stock, added to soups and stews, or sautéed. Overcooking makes it mushy. When it's just right it has the texture of a good young zucchini.

Cherimoya, sugar apple, bullock's heart, custard apple, anona (Latin American, Caribbean) A grapefruit-sized, yellowish-green fruit (reddish-brown when fully mature), heart-shaped and lumpy, containing a white, sweet, granular pulp with a custard-like consistency, and lots of glossy seeds. Cherimoyas are eaten raw with a spoon and make one of the world's best desserts. There is a fledgling U.S. production and the fruits are sometimes found in Latin American markets.

Cherry pepper (European) Cherry-sized and colored; these are often sold pickled in European delis. Some are mild and some are hot.

Chestnuts, kuri no kanro ni (Japanese, Chinese, European) Chestnuts are among the most globally widespread foods, though they are little used in the United States. They are more appreciated in Canada, but are still seldom seen there except roasted or in holiday stuffing. Elsewhere they show up as a vegetable, a dessert, and a pasta flour as well as in several other incarnations, bringing their beguilingly sweet taste and scent and characteristic mealy texture to all kinds of dishes. Fresh chestnuts sold in North America are often of poor quality, as the best ones do not get exported from their countries of origin. They also are available canned, both sweetened and plain; dried; and occasionally ground into flour (the luscious Italian *farina dolce*) or frozen whole. Chestnut flour is used to thicken Italian sauces and make various breads, pudding, cakes, and polenta. It makes wonderful cookies and sensational pasta. You can grind your own from dried chestnuts if you have a flour mill. The flour is perishable (and also expensive) and should be refrigerated and used within a month.

Korean chestnuts are popular fresh and dried, both in stews and sweets. The Japanese variety is most often sold in bottles and cans in heavy syrup.

———————— ✤ ————————

RECIPE: **Castagnaccio (Rough Chestnuts)**
The Chestnut Cook Book, p. 91. An ancient preparation (famine food, actually) that combines the irreducible tastes of Tuscany— olive oil, chestnuts, pine nuts, and grape.

    2 cups chestnut flour
    6 tablespoons olive oil, divided
    Pinch salt
    1 cup water
    small handful pine nuts
    small handful golden raisins
    1 sprig rosemary

Preheat oven to 325°F. Put flour in a bowl with 2 tablespoons oil and salt. Stir and slowly add water, mixing to eliminate lumps. Add enough water to form a thick batter or a thin dough. Pour into an 8-inch cake pan in which the remaining oil has been spread. Smooth down. Olive oil should creep up the sides and spill over the top. Press pine nuts, raisins, and rosemary into the top of the cake. Bake about 35 minutes. Serves 6–8.

Chicharrón (Latin American, Mexican) Fried pork rind. You can buy them bagged in Latin markets and many supermarkets, especially in the south. *Chicharrón* are sometimes flavored with paprika or stronger chiles. Besides being eaten as a snack, they are crumbled over a number of Mexican dishes as a seasoning.

Chile de árbol (Mexican, Latin American) Small, thin, cayenne-type peppers, generally sold red. The name refers to the shape of the plant, which resembles a small tree. Any thin-fleshed hot pepper can substitute.

Chile oil (Chinese, Thai, Malaysian) Sesame oil infused with hot dried chiles, which are discarded before bottling. It should be dark red. Used as a dipping oil or mixed with other oils for cooking. The hottest ones are from Thailand and Malaysia; milder varieties are Taiwanese and Chinese. Or you can make your own by adding dried, seeded chiles (serranos would be a good choice) to heated sesame oil and letting the covered mixture sit for a week or two. A bottle of chile oil I recently bought had a harsh, rather nasty flavor (I think the culprit was poor-quality oil) and I think I'll make my own next time.

Chiles If potatoes are the most basic gift of the New World, perhaps chiles are the most appreciated. Chile preferences are a red-hot subject, so to speak, and they evince as much passion as tastes in barbecue. It's also confusing for cooks who want to get the ingredients exactly right, since chile labeling is rife with local names and local varieties. Furthermore, fresh and dried chiles of the same variety often go by entirely different names. Names can be vague and generic, or almost too specific, such as the Yucatecan pepper sauce named "makes a dog's nose hot," and the Thai and Laotian favorite *khi nu,* which I'm told translates as "rat droppings."

Asian and African chiles all sprang originally from the Americas, but cross-breeding, both planned and impromptu, has developed local characteristics of size, shape, and flavor. It should be possible to match at least the basics you need at just about any non-European ethnic market. So if your community has a Mexican grocery but no Asian one (or vice versa), you can come close enough to the variety you want. Many varieties of dried chiles also are available by mail order and they are surprisingly easy to grow. Hot peppers will not develop their full power or flavor in cooler gardens, but they are quite hardy and will mature faster than their more delicate sweet cousins. I grow jalapeños and serranos yearly, within shouting distance of the Canadian border.

A few general tips: The bigger and thicker the pepper, the milder it is likely to be. The real screamers—tabascos, birdseye, habañeros, and so on—are small and thin. A jalapeño, more or less in the middle of the heat spectrum, is smallish, but comparatively thick fleshed. Some hot peppers have a rather vine-gary tang; others, such as habañeros, have a beguiling, almost floral underlying flavor. These fine points may be lost on the novice chile eater who is more concerned with varying degrees of pain, but veterans can enjoy the more subtle variations, and the pleasure of arguing them with others.

The wisdom of my youth was that the seeds are the hottest part, but it turns out that it's the membrane to which the seeds cling. So prepare your peppers accordingly.

Chiltepe chile (Central American) A tiny, "unimproved" chile, about the size of a pea, with an intense hot flavor, used fresh in salsas. Bird chile is an acceptable substitute.

Chinese okra, angled luffa, sze kwa, pleated squash, silk squash (Chinese) Common in Asian markets, this vegetable looks like a huge okra and tastes more like a soft cucumber. The younger the squash the better, as it gets bitter with age. It is used in soups and stir fries and can also be added to vegetable curries. Its own flavor is mild and pleasant, and its spongy texture soaks up other tastes. Peeling is unnecessary, but do cut off the ridges before slicing.

RECIPE REFERENCE: **Silk Squash and Fresh Mushroom Soup (Guah Sin Gu Tong),** *Chinese Vegetarian Cooking,* pp. 158–159.

Chinese sausage (Chinese, Pan-Asian) Firm, slender, slightly sweet sausage made mainly of pork liver. Also used in Vietnamese and Philippine cooking. Available fresh and frozen in Asian groceries and well-stocked supermarkets.

Chipiron (European) Highly concentrated packets of extract of cephalopods, such as octopus and squid, allow you to prepare

black rice and similar dishes without bringing the entire creature into your kitchen. Food author Paula Wolfert says that one
$1/2$-teaspoon packet will make a full recipe.

Chipotle (Mexican) A mature jalapeño pepper, with a sweeter, nut-
tier flavor than the fresh green ones. You may find chipotles
dried and smoked; more often they are sold in a tomato-based
sauce or pickled. See also, **jalapeño.** Chipolte salsas are gain-
ing popularity in many local supermarkets, a good way to try out
the flavor.

Chocolate chile (Central American) A medium-hot brown chile
about two inches long, grown in eastern Guatemala. This chile
is not to be confused with the big sweet "chocolate peppers"
sometimes found in groceries and at farmers' markets, which
are a variant on your basic green pepper.

Chufa, earth chestnut, tiger nut, earth almond (Mexican, Central American, Spanish) A small starchy tuber sold dried in
Latin American markets and used to make the popular sweet
drink *horchata de chufa,* a whitish mixture somewhat like almond milk. Chufas also can be eaten out of hand.

Chui (Korean) A wild mountain green, with a flavor between
spinach and watercress, which is sometimes found dried in Korean markets. It is used in soups.

Cilantro, coriander, cilantrillo, yuen sai, kinchay, pak chee
(Chinese, Pan-Asian, Indian, Latin American, European, Mid-
dle Eastern) Essential to dishes in Central and South America,
China, North Africa, and India, and increasingly familiar to
North Americans as the distinctive flavor in salsa, both red and
green. The dried seeds are sold whole and ground as coriander.

Thai cooks also use the cilantro root in soups and black bean/meat dishes. The delicate, often lacy leaves have an unmistakable flavor, sort of smoky mint, when fresh. Dried cilantro is available but virtually tasteless. Cilantro doesn't keep well. If you have to buy in quantity, it's best to use it up in a big batch of salsa, or steep it in boiling water to make coriander water, which can be frozen and used as flavoring when the real thing is not available. Or you can purée the leaves and freeze the resulting mush in an ice-cube tray. If you have any garden space at all you can grow your own, as it is remarkably tolerant of both heat and cold. Be sure to buy seed marked especially for leaf production rather than for coriander seed. Otherwise your plants will bolt to seed as soon as they come out of the ground. See also **Coriander** and **Eryngium**.

Cloud ears, tree ears, wood ears, silver ears, black fungus, kikurage, mogi posot (Chinese, Japanese, Pan-Asian) A strangely textured mushroom, simultaneously soft and crunchy, with a mild flavor, nearly always sold dried. They are familiar to lovers of hot and sour soup, where they are a counterpoint to the brisk flavors that predominate. The best-quality mushrooms are whole rather than broken. They should be soaked in warm water before cooking. There are a number of varieties. Wood ears are the biggest and darkest; silver ears are smaller and paler and appear in one of the more unusual Chinese dishes, a soup featuring mushrooms simmered in a syrup of rock sugar and orange juice.

Coban chiles (Latin American) Popular in Guatemala, these are small round balls, about $1/2$ inch in diameter. They get their characteristic smoky taste from being dried over a wood fire.

Coconut (Pan-Asian, Caribbean, Latin American) Coconut palms
provide food, drink, and cooking oil, plus the shelter under
which to cook them, for millions of people in the tropics. In
parts of Southeast Asia coconut is a staple second only to rice.
Only a fraction of the incarnations of this versatile plant are
available for export. Although tourists may have learned the
pleasure of drinking the sweet juice from a young coconut, before the flesh has hardened and pulled flavor from the liquid,
few are familiar with the gradations the nuts go through on the
way to becoming the fully ripe, often overaged specimens that
show up in northern supermarkets. It makes fascinating reading, beyond the scope of this guide. I recommend the section in
Sri Owen's *Indonesian Regional Cooking*.

The juice of young coconuts is used as a cooking liquid in the
countries where it is easily obtainable. One odd-sounding substitute, certified by the respected Vietnamese chef Binh Duong,
is the coconut soda pop sold in many ethnic groceries. (This is
not to say, however, that the soda pop itself reproduces the divine flavor of the real thing.) The basics of coconut cuisine generally available to North American cooks are mature coconut
flesh and coconut milk. If you want to make your own coconut
milk from scratch, several good cookbooks will tell you how.
The first, richest pressing is used for thick curry sauces, and is
sometimes put in coffee. Second and third pressings are more
appropriate as marinades and as a cooking liquid for meats and
vegetables.

The array of convenience products in ethnic markets should
serve as a clue that most cooks, even traditional ones, don't al-

ways make the milk themselves. You can bet that Thai restaura-
teurs are not hand-processing all the coconut milk for all that
green shrimp curry. Coconut milk is available canned, frozen,
and dried. The frozen milk (Mendonca's is one popular brand
name) comes in containers like frozen orange juice and probably tastes the closest to fresh-made. It contains no preservatives
and should be used within a day of mixing. Canned varieties are
cheap and have a bit more staying power. Powdered coconut
milk is available in many stores; it has the advantage of allowing you to mix up exact amounts to order. Some brands are
presweetened, though, and not suitable for many recipes, so
shop with care. Low-fat coconut milk (something of an oxy-
moron) is also beginning to get shelf space. The flavor is okay
to my taste, but recipes requiring long cooking may be affected
by the reduction in oil.

Coconut milk changes as it cooks. First it becomes thick and
smooth, provided that it is stirred continuously, in a down-up-
and-over motion to prevent curdling. (This thickened liquid is
the beginning stage for many of the canned varieties, especially
those labeled "coconut cream.") Do not cover, as you want the
excess water to evaporate. If it does start to separate into solids
and water, you can generally reunite its elements by stirring in
a bit more thick coconut milk. If cooking continues, the milk
will continue to thicken and will eventually separate into an oil
and a semisolid residue at the bottom of the pan. The residue,
called *blondo* in Indonesia and used in sauces and sambals, can
be collected when it is still white, or further cooked to a golden
brown, depending on the recipe. The oil is widely used in

Southeast Asian cooking. One Indonesian technique makes use of all the stages of this process. The main ingredient (traditionally buffalo, but also beef, beans, or a starchy vegetable such as unripe jackfruit) is simmered for hours in spiced coconut milk until the water is evaporated, and then is transferred to a wok to fry in the remaining oil. (See *Indonesian Regional Cooking,* pp. 40–42.)

Coconut flesh also comes in many convenience forms. The moist, sweetened "angel flake" style sold in supermarkets is not suitable for most Asian or Indian recipes, although it does show up in some Philippine desserts. Unsweetened dried coconut is abundant and cheap in Asian and Indian groceries. It is generally sold in several sizes, from finely grated to big flakes. Unlike the highly modified supermarket stuff, unsweetened flakes go rancid easily and will then ruin whatever dish they touch. Sniff before buying and keep cool and dry. Frozen grated coconut is also increasingly available (Yaco is a popular brand) and is the closest thing to having a backyard tree. Both the dried and frozen varieties can be roasted to bring out the flavor. You want to start out with moist flakes, so thaw the frozen varieties or soak the dried ones before cooking. To make coconut butter, which is called for in some Southeast Asian recipes, first roast the grated coconut in a heavy skillet at low heat, stirring constantly, until brown. Remove from heat and grind to a smooth paste. See also **Macapuno.**

RECIPE: Coconut Chutney

> 1 cup grated coconut (fresh, frozen or dried and soaked)
> 1 tablespoon pan-roasted garbanzo flour
> 2 serranos or other small, hot chiles, seeded, and
>   chopped fine
> 1 inch ginger, chopped fine
> 3 tablespoons chopped cilantro
> $^1/_4$ teaspoon asefetida
> 2 tablespoons lemon juice or $^1/_2$ cup yogurt
> salt to taste

Combine all ingredients and serve with rice or dal. Makes about 1 $^1/_2$ cup.

———————————— ✌ ————————————

Cocum (Indian) Grown on the west coast of India, cocum is a dark purple fruit with a large seed. Like tamarind, it gives a sour aspect to fish and legume curries and also provides a pale purple color. It is used to make sherbets and cold drinks as well.

Coriander seed, dhania, sookha, kothamalie (Sinhalese) (Middle Eastern, Indian, European) Little light, round seeds of the aromatic cilantro plant. They are mildly spicy, nothing like coriander leaves in smell or taste. Whole seeds are used in pickling. The ground spice is used in many baked goods, masalas, soups, and so on. See also **Cilantro.**

Couscous (North African) The name refers to both the specialty pasta and the famous dish made from it. It is the national dish of Algeria, Morocco, and Tunisia and there are close to an infinite number of varieties. Its origins are uncertain, although food historian Copeland Marks favors the theory that the basic technique was developed in Sicily and brought from there to North Africa when Muslim families were forced to flee around 1400.

Beyond the hundreds of "authentic" couscous dishes, in recent years there has been an explosion of convenience versions: couscous in a cup, instant couscous, and other quick fixes. Although the full process is hardly fast food, it is not particularly difficult, and the fluffy texture and blend of flavors are well worth a bit of effort. Couscous is made from moistened semolina (the dough made from the endosperm of durum wheat) rolled into tiny pellets and dried. Individual dishes and approaches vary, but basically, the couscous gets its moist lightness from alternate steaming and soaking, allowing the water-resistant semolina to gradually take on moisture and also pick up flavor from the steaming stock beneath. If you are a regular couscous cook, you will surely get a *couscousière* for the steaming. But it is easy enough to improvise: I use a fine-mesh colander suspended over a saucepan, with a towel wrapped around the gap between lid and pot.

Here's how you do it. Start by rinsing the couscous. Drain, toss to distribute the moisture, and spread out on a tray for 10–15 minutes. Break up any clumps with your finger, put the couscous in your steamer, and steam over simmering water or stock for 30 minutes. Put the couscous in a bowl and sprinkle with liquid (water, stock, or milk, depending on the recipe) and let stand. Different recipes recommend a standing time of as short as 10 minutes or as long as an hour. If you moistened your couscous with plain water, you should now toss it with a little olive oil. Return to steamer and steam another 10–20 minutes. Some recipes will now have you repeat this process with more liquid, a longer absorption time, and yet another steaming. It is done when the grain has expanded to about three times its original size and is light and fluffy. Instant couscous has been steamed to this point and then redried. It's quick and it's edible, but it isn't the same.

Curry leaf, daun kari, neem, kah lee yip, karapincha, karuveppilai karapincha (Indian, Chinese, Pan-Asian) A fragrant herb that can be fried in the initial stages of a curry or simmered later. It looks like a skinny bay leaf and has a sweet/spicy flavor. It needs to cook at least 5 minutes. Curry leaf is used in dals, *khadis,* and yogurt and vegetable dishes, as well as the sambals and curries of Sri Lanka. Sometimes it's available fresh in Indian and Middle Eastern markets. The dried *neem* sold in Indian markets is best avoided, but if you must buy it dried, a spicy odor is a good sign. Curry leaf is not the same as the lacy-leaved curry plant, whose leaves smell a bit like grocery store curry powder.

D

Daikon, labanos, mooli lobahk (Japanese, Chinese, Pan-Asian) A big, mild white radish, daikon looks like a huge, ungainly white carrot and provides the image for the descriptive Hawaiian insult "daikon leg." (Some sources distinguish between daikon and *mooli,* but if not identical, they are close enough as to be interchangeable.) Daikon is ubiquitous in Japanese cooking, sold fresh, pickled and dried. One variety, Miyashigi, is sweeter than most and is grown especially for drying. Once dried and shredded it is called *kiri-boshi daikon* and is used, after soaking and braising, as a side vegetable dish. Fresh daikon should be crisp, with no brown or soft spots. It is common raw in salads and fresh pickles, and braised, stir-fried, or added to soups and kimchee. The pickled varieties range from tangy to quite sweet.

RECIPE: Braised Daikon
Winter Harvest, p. 179.

> 1 1/2 pounds fresh daikon, peeled and diced
> 2 tablespoons light cooking oil
> 1 teaspoon sugar
> 1 1/2 tablespoons soy sauce
> 1/4 cup water

Put daikon in a saucepan, cover with water, and bring to a boil. Boil for about 5 minutes, drain, and set aside. Heat a skillet or heavy saucepan, add oil and stir-fry daikon for 2 minutes. Add sugar and soy sauce. Stir and mix for another minute so that the sugar and soy coat the daikon. Add water, cover, and bring to boil. Reduce heat to medium-low and cook about 30 minutes or until daikon is tender but not mushy. Stir occasionally to keep daikon coated with sauce. Serve hot. Serves 4.

Dal (Indian) A generic term for "legume," dal is among the most important forms of Indian cooking (and perhaps least appreciated by outsiders), providing protein, a sauce for rice, a dip for bread, and a vehicle for flavors ranging from the most subtle of spiced butters to the most complex and fiery spices. For me the transition from my mother's famous lentil soup to the spicy purées of Indian cooking was an easy one, and I have hardly ever met a dal I didn't like. The most common dals are varieties of lentil, which are favored because they are quick-cooking and easy to digest, but beans and dried peas are also widely used. Dals follow the rule of other Indian dishes. Those served in the north to be eaten with bread tend to be thick; those made in the south to be eaten with rice are thinner, more soupy. Any Indian grocery will have a bewildering array of dals, whole and split, hulled and not, some coated with oil and others simply dry. *Toor dal* and *masoor dal* make good starting points for a novice dal cook. Any imported dal should be picked over for extraneous rocks and other junk, and then rinsed thoroughly before using. (See individual varieties for more information.)

RECIPE REFERENCE: **Sambhar Masala**, *Flatbreads and Flavors*, pp. 153–154. *A South Indian preparation, made with dal and used to spice more dal.*

Dang myun (Korean) The Korean version of bean thread noodles—thin, grayish tan, made from potato and sweet potato starch. The noodles should be soaked in boiling water before use in soups and stir fries.

Dhansak masala (Indian) A combination of sweet and hot spices that alludes to the Persian ancestry of India's Parsi ethnic group, melded with their long residence in the Gujarat, on the chile-loving western coast of the subcontinent. *Dhansak masala* is used on meat, vegetable, and lentil curries. Some Indian groceries carry it. Otherwise you can approximate the flavor with $1^1/2$ teaspoons of *garam masala,* $^1/4$ teaspoon star anise powder, and $^1/4$ teaspoon nutmeg.

Dibs rumman, hamod er rumman, pomegranate molasses, grenadine syrup (Middle Eastern, Turkish) Concentrated syrup distilled from pomegranate fruit. It is available in Middle Eastern groceries and is used to obtain the sweet/sour flavor popular in soups, chicken, and vegetable dishes. This is one of my favorite new discoveries of this book, the perfect tangy touch for a dish of lentils or a chicken marinade as well as in the many recipes which call for it, such as the Iraqi soup *shawrbat rumman* (Shawrbat means liquid, *rumman* means pomegrante) with ground meat, onion, cumin, cayenne, olive oil, cilantro, garlic, scallions, mint, lentils, tarragon, and chile powder. (See *The Arabian Delights Cookbook,* p. 48.)

Diente de perro chile (Guatemalan) About one inch long and shaped like a canine tooth—hence the name—bright red and hot. This chile is similar to the beloved Thai and Indonesian bird chile, and they can be used interchangeably. See also **Pequin chile**.

Dim sum (Chinese) *Dim sum* (one translation is "delight the senses") are my idea of the perfect Sunday brunch. My husband and I used to sleep in, then wander down to the King Street Cafe in Seattle and join the multigenerational Chinese families in trying out as many kinds as we could hold. We wouldn't stagger out until the table was piled with stacks of little plates, which the waiters counted to total up the bill. Besides my personal nostalgia and their wonderful flavors, *dim sum* illustrate dozens of ingenious ways to make a pastry without using an oven. Some of the most popular, available to go from many Asian markets, are listed here.

Siu mai A steamed minced pork dumpling wrapped in a wonton skin. This is a popular Chinese breakfast dish. The highest-quality ones also include shrimp.

Ngau yuk siu mai Same as *siu mai,* with beef instead of pork.

Ha gau Lightly cooked shrimp in a translucent curved wheat starch wrapper. *Ha* means "shrimp" and *gow* means "crescent."

Fun gau Shrimp, pork, mushrooms and bamboo shoots in a half moon–shaped wheat starch wrapper

Pai gwat Pork spareribs with barbecue sauce or sour plum sauce.

Cheung fun A rice flour roll filled with barbecued pork, shrimp, or beef, topped with sweet scallion oil.

Cha siu bau Barbecued pork in a soft wheat bun. This is one of the most famous Cantonese dishes.

Siu loon bau A Shanghai dumpling filled with soup and minced pork and shrimp; served with finely shredded young ginger and red vinegar dipping sauce. The trick is to mix the soup with agar-agar and let it jell. Then cut the gelatin into chunks to fill the thin dumplings. When they are steamed, the heated gelatin will liquefy inside its covering.

Nor mai A steamed lotus leaf packet of sticky rice, chicken, sausage, pork, and black mushrooms.

Yung dau fu Fresh tofu stuffed with shrimp.

Woo gok An egg-shaped deep-fried croquette of mashed taro root stuffed with a minced mixture of pork, shrimp, mushrooms, and bamboo shoots.

Cheung guen A spring roll.

Jien dui A chewy, sweet sesame seed ball filled with red bean paste.

Hom soi gok A sticky rice flour dumpling filled with minced pork, shrimp, bamboo shoots, and black mushrooms.

Lo bok goh Pan-fried squares of radish pudding cake.

Mah tai goh Pan-fried squares of sweet water chestnut pudding cake.

Dried scallops, conpoy, gong yew chew (Chinese, Pan-Asian) These look like amber-colored poker chips, about an inch in diameter and half an inch thick. They are heavily salted and strongly flavored with a bit of sweetness, and are used to add interest to simple vegetable dishes, soups, and congees. They must be soaked before use. Overnight soaking with a bit of sherry is recommended for soups and braised dishes; at least two hours is best for stir fries, followed by a few minutes of steaming. Shred before using. You may also find dried oysters, abalone, and squid. Soaking time is related to original toughness; that is, abalone and squid need more soaking than scallops and oysters. Dried squid are particularly popular in Asia. Called *ojingo* in Korea, they are favored either raw or toasted over an open flame as a popular snack food. The Vietnamese taste is similar; dried squid are often eaten alternately with bites of fresh pineapple. Abalone is sold both canned and dried in Asian markets. Like fresh abalone, the reconstituted dried abalone should be cooked either very briefly at a high temperature or gently for a long time. Halfway measures result in a texture that is like chewing on an inner tube.

RECIPE REFERENCE: **Braised dried scallops and radishes,** *The Thousand Recipe Chinese Cookbook*, Gloria Bley Miller, p. 489

Dried shrimp roe (Japanese) Little reddish grains, very salty and strong flavored. Used as a condiment over mild dishes.

Durian (Pan-Asian) Definitely a cult item (it has its own Internet website—http://www.ecst.csuchico.edu/~durian) as well as a popular fruit in much of Southeast Asia, durian (*Durio zibethinus*) is either alluring or disgusting, depending in large part on your reaction to its smell. In a closed space it can be overpowering. Chef Andy Pforzheimer writes that it's "like eating pudding in an outhouse." The fruit is green, about cantaloupe sized, but lumpier, with fierce-looking spines. It is really ugly. Durians are tied to the trees as they ripen, to keep them from falling and getting bruised and to avoid braining those below. The pale yellow interior is in banana-shaped sections, soft and creamy, sometimes likened in texture to raw brains. Durian is sold frozen, canned, and candied as well as fresh, and can be found in many Asian markets. Cookbooks tend to contain many awed references but few actual recipes, but Sri Owen, who also provides the least hysterical description I have read of durian in her book *Indonesian Regional Cooking*, does mention *nasi ketan*, a dessert of black glutinous rice, coconut milk, and "slightly overripe" durian. If the full durian experience is more than you want to tackle, you can also buy bottled artificial durian flavoring.

ᵉᵍ E ᵍᵉ

Egusi (African) Seeds of the African "watermelon," a small round fruit with pink or white flesh, which is actually a squash and is cultivated in western and central Africa. The small, pale, flattish seeds are eaten as a snack, either plain or toasted with a little oil, salt, and chile. Ground and mixed to a paste, they are used to thicken stews and soups. They are often mixed with ground black pepper into cakes sold as seasoning mix. *Egusi* seeds are sold ground and whole in African markets, or sesame seed meal can be used as a substitute.

RECIPE: **Spinach Pudding**
A West African Cookbook, p. 95.

> $1/2$ pound smoked fish
> water
> 1 pound fresh spinach or mixed greens, finely chopped
> 1 medium onion, peeled and chopped
> $1/2$ cup *egusi* meal, divided
> 4 tablespoons peanut butter
> crushed red pepper to taste
> $1/2$ teaspoon salt

Cover smoked fish with water to soak. Boil $2 1/2$ cups water and add greens. Add onion and 2 tablespoons of the *egusi* meal. Reduce heat to medium, cover, and cook about 10 minutes. Mix the rest of the *egusi* meal with about $1/2$ cup water to make a thin paste and let stand. Rinse fish and cut into 4 or 5 pieces. Add to greens. Mix in peanut butter with enough hot liquid from the cooking pot to make a smooth gravy and add to the pan. Add pepper, salt, and *egusi* meal paste. Stir to blend and continue simmering, uncovered, for 45 minutes or until it thickens. Serves 4.

———————— ✌﹩ ————————

Egyptian rice (North African) A short grained, roundish, semi-glutinous rice that is used for pudding and for stuffed vegetables. *Arborio* rice is a fine substitute and Cal Rose or similar U.S. varieties are certainly acceptable.

Enokidake enoki (Japanese) Slender white mushrooms, sold fresh in clumps and canned. The tops should be white and fresh-looking. It's okay for the bottoms to be slippery and brown. They are often sold canned, but they lose their delicate aroma in the process, so use fresh ones if possible.

Epazote, wormseed, Jerusalem oak (Latin American) A large herb with a robust tang that is a signature taste of the cooking of southern Mexico and the Yucatán. It is also used in enchiladas and other dishes in Michoacan and points north. It grows well in northern latitudes, but does not keep well and is seldom sold fresh. If you do find fresh *epazote,* you will know it by its intense minty smell and thin, dark-green serrated leaves. The dried leaves are often found in Latin American markets; unlike many herbs, however, the dried is nowhere near as pungent as the fresh. *Epazote* is a member of the goosefoot (*Chenopodium*) family and is sometimes called by that name, but its flavor is different from that of the common goosefoot found in vacant lots and garden plots. It also is a relative of quinoa. See also **Quinoa**.

————————— ⚜ —————————

RECIPE: Caldo de Heuvo para la Goma
False Tongues and Sunday Bread. Egg soup for a hangover, from San Pedro Ayampuc, Guatemala, p. 83.

> 2 cups water
> $1/2$ teaspoon or more fresh hot chiles, chopped
> $1/4$ cup tomato, chopped
> 2 scallions, green part only, chopped
> $1/2$ cup fresh epazote leaves, chopped
> salt to taste
> 2 eggs

Bring water to a boil and add chiles, tomato, scallions, epazote, and salt. Simmer 15 minutes.

Drop eggs into soup and poach until firm, about 10 minutes. Don't break the yolks. Serve hot. Serves 2.

————————————————

Eryngium, eryngo, false coriander, ngo gai, saw leaf herb, thorny coriander, Puerto Rican coriander (Thai, Vietnamese, Caribbean, Mexican) A relative of parsley and of the odd-looking edible plant sea holly, this has tough, serrated leaves that smell and taste similar to cilantro, which is a fine substitute though a bit milder. It is used as a garnish in Vietnamese *pho,* and in some Thai salads and fish dishes.

✌ F ✌

Fava bean, fool, ful, foul, sora mame, tsan tau, horse bean, broad bean, bajilla (North African, Middle Eastern, African,

Japanese, Chinese, European, Mexican) Favas are an ancient bean variety (*Vicia faba*), originating in Europe and introduced to the Americas in the sixteenth century. Unlike New World beans, they are productive in cool weather. Favas have a rich, meaty flavor and can grow to enormous size; this combination made them popular for centuries as Lenten food in Catholic countries. They are sold fresh, canned, puréed, and dried, both in and out of the shell. Favas are used fresh in soups and salads; they are used dried in other soups, in *ful mudammas*, and mixed with chickpeas in some falafel recipes. Fresh young favas, in their pods, are used in North African couscous dishes. One Algerian example is *messouf*, where young favas and green beans are steamed with couscous and served with buttermilk on the side. The most common use of favas is in *ful mudammas*, the traditional Egyptian breakfast porridge sold by street vendors all along the Nile Valley. When made with the small, dark favas, this has a heavy, earthy flavor with a slight bite. Fresh favas come in huge flat pods, up to eighteen inches long, and should be firm and dark green. Dried ones range from small to huge, from pale to dark brown. Follow recipe instructions as to type. Eating undercooked beans or breathing the pollen is poisonous to some people of Mediterranean ancestry who are sensitive to vicine and convicine. Don't mess with this possibility. It can give you a serious form of anemia. In addition, some people have allergic reactions to the pods.

Fenugreek, methi (Indian, Middle Eastern, African) In South Indian cuisine, *methi* seeds are the second ingredient after mustard seeds to be put in hot oil and fried a few seconds. They are also roasted and powdered for the hot spice mixture *muligapuri*. The plant, occasionally found fresh in Indian markets, is a small legume, and the rock-hard seeds are a sort of tiny pea. They have a burnt sugar flavor that is not very appealing alone, but adds an essential note to many curries and chutneys as well as to North African dishes. Cooking softens the seeds so you don't lose a filling. The slightly bitter leaves are sometimes used in fresh chutneys and in South Indian dishes such as *methi aloo* and chicken *makhani*. The leaves are sold dried as *kasuri methi*. Fenugreek is also the main flavoring in imitation maple syrup. Yemeni cooks feature fenugreek in the traditional spice mixture *hulbah*, where it is powdered and mixed with garlic, onion, tomatoes, and pepper and then steeped in boiling water. Amharic-speaking Ethiopians add it to their sublime spice bread, along with coriander and cardamom.

Fermented black soy beans (Chinese) Soft, salty and pungent black soybeans; kind of a solid soy sauce, with a smoky flavor. These are the basis for black bean sauce, which also can be purchased bottled in Asian markets. A standard use is with spareribs, but I like it even better on seafood. The beans are sold canned or in plastic bags. A little goes a long way, but they keep forever so none need go to waste.

———————— ✌ ————————

RECIPE: **Black Bean Calamari**
Winter Harvest, pp. 149–150. Originally provided by John Kemnitzer.

4 tablespoons cooking oil
1 cup carrots, julienned
1 cup celery, julienned
$^1/_2$ cup turnips, julienned (optional)
1 pound squid, cleaned and cut into $^1/_2$-inch rings
1 cup black bean sauce, or more to taste
$^1/_4$ cup green onions, sliced
1 teaspoon black sesame seeds, lightly toasted
1 teaspoon white sesame seeds, lightly toasted
Black bean sauce:
$3^1/_2$ cups water, divided
$^1/_2$ cup fermented black beans
$^1/_2$ cup plus 3 tablespoons sake or dry white wine,
    divided
1 tablespoon minced garlic
$^1/_2$ cup soy sauce
4 teaspoons Sichuan paste
$^1/_2$ tablespoon sesame oil
$^1/_2$ tablespoon fresh ginger, minced
2 tablespoons sugar
pinch crushed red chile pepper
$^3/_4$ teaspoon ground Sichuan pepper
$^3/_4$ teaspoon Chinese five-spice powder
3 tablespoons cornstarch

For the squid: Heat oil in a medium skillet until it just begins to smoke. Add carrots, celery, and turnips (if used) and toss for 30 seconds or until vegetables just begin to cook. Add squid and cook, tossing, until rings start to turn opaque, 1 minute at most. [This is important; eating over-cooked squid is like eating rubber bands.] Add black bean sauce and toss until sauce is hot, about 30 seconds. Garnish with green onions and sesame seeds.

For the black bean sauce: Bring 1 $1/2$ cups water to a boil and add black beans. Simmer 5 minutes. Strain and discard the water. Retain about a quarter of the beans for texture and purée the rest. Combine the remaining 2 cups water, $1/2$ cup of the sake and all remaining ingredients except cornstarch in a saucepan and bring to a boil. Add beans and return to boiling. Reduce heat to simmer. Combine cornstarch and remaining 3 tablespoons sake in a small bowl. Add slowly to black beans, whisking to mix thoroughly. Simmer gently for 5 minutes. Serves 4, with 1 cup extra bean sauce to save for other meals.

Fig leaves (Mediterranean) Turkish cooks use them to wrap fish or poultry for grilling. Grape leaves can be substituted.

Fish sauce nam pla, nam padek, shottsuru (Asian) One of the oldest savory flavoring mixtures recorded, fish sauce was a common ingredient during the Roman Empire, with many sages and writers weighing in on the virtues of various fish species and methods of preparation. The taste for *garum* went where the Roman legions went, showing up as both an ingredient and a table seasoning. Often made with mackerel, *garum* was flavored with herbs or mixed with concentrated grape juice or wine. Traces of that flavoring idea remain in the many Italian recipes involving salted anchovies cooked in a sweet-and-sour mixture, and in Great Britain in the form of Worcestershire sauce. Basically, fish—saltwater, fresh, or a mixture of both—are salted, mixed with water, and allowed to ferment, generally in wooden casks. The resultant liquid is clear, light to dark brown in color, salty, and fishy-smelling.

The sauce apparently was invented independently in Asia, where the primary fish sauce cuisines are those of Vietnam, Thailand, Cambodia, Laos, and to a lesser extent, Myanmar (formerly Burma) and the Philippines. Other products commonly added to the fish sauce seasonings are coconut, onion, garlic, lemongrass, ginger, lemon or lime juice, cilantro, peanuts, and chile pepper. The characteristic common to all fish sauces is its surprisingly light taste, almost sweet as an aftertaste, in contrast to its rank smell. Within that general pattern there are regional variations. Vietnamese fish sauce is the most delicate and the lightest in color. Laotian is stronger and sometimes contains chunks of the fermented fish. See individual names.

Five-spice powder (Chinese) Long storied for its flavor and medicinal properties, and for the cosmological value of the number five, this famous condiment actually comes in a number of varieties. It always contains star anise and cinnamon or cassia, to give the characteristic blend of licorice and sweet/hot flavor. Beyond that you may find Sichuan pepper, fennel, fennel seed, cloves, licorice root, or ginger. It is good as a dipping condiment and with grilled meats such as the Cantonese favorite, crispy skin pork.

Fuzzy melon, mo kwa (Chinese) Kind of like a fat zucchini, but pale green and spongy. The flavor is nice, mild and compatible with stronger flavors. It is used in soups and stir fries. Fuzzy melon is related to the larger winter melon, and similar in its uses.

◆§ G §◆

Gadeed, gargoosh (North African, Middle Eastern) Thin slices of sun-dried meat from North Africa and the Middle East. Lamb and camel are frequent sources, but good quality beef jerky can be substituted. See also **Carne seca**.

Galangal, laos, languas, ka, kencur, Siamese ginger, aromatic ginger (Pan-Asian) A cousin to ginger with a crisper texture, a pinkish color, and a somewhat milder, less mustardy flavor. It is much used in Southeast Asian curries and soups; if you have fallen in love with Thai or Cambodian soups, you probably are a galangal fan already. It is sold fresh in Asian markets, looking like a thicker, more symmetrical version of ginger. Dried slices are also usable, though not as good. Soak them in cold water before cooking and remove before the dish goes to the table. Try to avoid the powdered form; it is indistinguishable from ginger, so why pay more? Some books and some cooks distinguish between galangal and *laos*; some say they are interchangeable. Certainly they are similar.

————————————— ❧ —————————————

RECIPE: **Peanut Butter Sambal**
Dishes from Indonesia, p. 42–43.

>   2 fresh whole chiles
>   2 onions, quartered
> $1/4$ teaspoon galangal or ginger, chopped
>   1 teaspoon brown sugar
>   2 tablespoons tamarind juice
>   1 teaspoon lemon rind, grated
>   1 small piece grilled shrimp paste
>   2 tablespoons water
>   1 cup crunchy peanut butter or ground roasted peanuts
>   salt

Stir-fry chiles and onions until soft. Place in blender with galangal, brown sugar, tamarind juice, lemon rind, shrimp paste, and water. Mix with peanuts and salt to taste. Dilute with hot water as needed. Makes $1 1/2$ cups.

————————————— ❧ —————————————

Garbanzo bean, chickpea, ceci bean, babuli canna, safaid channa, nohut (Turkish) (European, North African, Middle Eastern, Indian) Big, roundish, rich-tasting dried peas—the base for hummus, not to mention that picnic and potluck standby, three bean salad. Garbanzos are much used in Mediterranean soups. Their oddest manifestation may be the ones sold in sweet syrup to make the Philippine parfait dessert *halohalo,* which also features purple *ube* yam and canned corn—a strange combination, but very popular. Garbanzos take a long time to cook, which is one reason it's nice that they are widely available canned. Smaller black hulled chickpeas, called *kala channa,* are sold in Indian markets, as are their hulled counterparts, *channa dal.* See also **Channa dal.**

Garbanzo flour, gram flour, besan (Indian, North African, Middle Eastern, European) Actually we are talking about two sources here—the Indian version is made from a smaller bean than the European garbanzo, but the flavor is the same. Ground dried garbanzo beans make a very fine, pale yellow flour that looks like masa but has (to me anyway) a somewhat unpleasant smell. That is quickly remedied in cooking, however, where it is versatile and delicious. Used in Indian *pakoras* and other deep-fried treats (including the red-hot Ramzat, a popular packaged snack sold in many Indian groceries) and as a thickener for vegetable curries. Around the Mediterranean it is more often baked into a breadlike snack sold as street food. *Socca* (see recipe) is more like a crepe; *karantika,* an Algerian version including eggs and flavored with cumin, is thicker, a sort of cross between a quick bread and a pudding.

RECIPE: Socca

> 1 cup chickpea flour
> 1 cup water
> 3 tablespoons olive oil, divided
> pinch salt

Mix flour, water, olive oil and salt to make a thin batter. Let the mixture stand an hour and then pour into an ovenproof pan. Batter should very barely cover the bottom. Broil at 400°F about 15 minutes, sprinkling on some more olive oil at the halfway point. Serve warm or at room temperature. This is unbelievably good for such a simple dish.

Genmai cha (Japanese) Green tea with roasted rice kernels. It has a nice, earthy, smoky flavor. Store in an airtight container.

Ghee, semneh (Indian, Arabic) Clarified butter made by melting unsalted butter and straining it to remove any sediment and the white foam that contains the remaining milk solids. The remaining purified butterfat will keep without refrigeration, has a mild flavor, and resists burning. *Ghee* simply means "fat," and ghee from butter is properly called *usli ghee.* As middle-class Indians have come to share Western worries about saturated fats, many have turned to light cooking oils instead, and so may you, although the flavor of spices cooked in ghee is memorable. A vegetable shortening colored and flavored to resemble ghee, called *vanaspati ghee,* also has gained popularity in India as the price of butter has risen. Both ghees are available in Indian groceries. The vegetable version costs half as much as butter ghee, but it is simple enough to make your own at home and save both the money and the flavor. Spiced and/or slightly fermented versions of ghee are regional specialties. See **Nitter kibbeh** and **Smen**.

Ginkgo nuts, bok guah, unhaeng (Chinese, Korean) Small oval nuts with hard shells. Fresh nuts are pale green and need to be cooked. Simmer them for 30 minutes, then add cold water to cool. They are easy to skin once cooked. Canned nuts are translucent and already cooked, ready to use. Raw nuts will keep, refrigerated, about a month. Once cooked they are good for a few days. These are used as a garnish for Korean party dishes.

RECIPE REFERENCE: **Buddha's Delight** (a traditional New Year's dish), *From the Earth: Chinese Vegetarian Cooking,* p. 101.

Ginseng, insam (Korean, Chinese) Besides its reputation as a restorative in herbal medicine, ginseng root is used in Korea as a vegetable pickle. Fresh young white rootlets are dressed in a chile and vinegar sauce, or sliced and eaten raw, dipped in honey. Ginseng is also added to cooked dishes, such as *samgyae tang*—chicken stuffed with glutinous rice—and some Chinese soups. Dried ginseng can be reconstituted if fresh is not available. Ginseng tea, the best known Western use, is called *insam-cha.*

Glutinous rice, sticky rice, sweet rice, mochi-gomé (Asian) A usually short-grained rice with a slightly sweet flavor and lot of amylopectin, a gelatinizing component that helps hold the grains together. The amount of amylopectin determines whether rice is sticky or not. Long-grain rice of the American and Indian types has very little. Japanese and *arborio* rices have a fair amount, and East Asian sticky rice has a lot. Long soaking before a brief cooking helps to release the sticky aspect. Although the most familiar types are white and short-grained, sticky rice can be red or even black, and there are long-grain varieties as well. Sometimes glutinous rice is flaked into thin slices and dyed a pale green. It may not say so on the label, but this type has been parboiled as well as flattened for quick cooking and maximum stickiness. It is used in puddings and other sweets, often cooked with coconut milk, and also to stuff poultry. Check labels carefully because the wrong type can ruin a dish. See also **rice flour**.

Golden needles, dried lily buds (Chinese) These are the unopened flowers of the evanescent day lily, used in *mu shu* pork, hot and sour soup, and many stir fries. One eminent Chinese chef describes the taste as "moldy," but I like them. They should be golden and flexible rather than dark and brittle. Soak before cooking.

Goma abura (Japanese, Chinese) Dark sesame oil, used as a condiment and added in small quantities to flavor vegetable oil for deep frying. Do not use it alone in cooking, as the flavor is too strong.

Goreng bawang, fried onions (Indonesian, Thai, Chinese, Indian) Golden, crisp fried onions, used as a garnish in lots of Indonesian and Thai recipes. They are made with the dry shallotlike onion common in Southeast Asia, which fries up more easily than the big, watery European types. They are crunchy, with a mild onion flavor and a slight bitter edge. The ones I buy are from Taiwan; besides their use in Asian cooking, they are the perfect garnish for a tomato and mayo sandwich on toasted multigrain bread.

RECIPE: **Nasi Gurih**
Dishes from Indonesia, p. 22.

> 3 cups oval-grain rice (*arborio* or Cal Rose are good
>   choices)
> 4 cups coconut milk
> 2 *salam* leaves
> ¹/₂ teaspoon salt
> 1 cup fried onions

Rinse rice in cold water. Drain. Pour coconut milk into a
medium saucepan. Add *salam* leaves and salt and bring to a boil,
uncovered, stirring constantly. Add rice and stir very briefly with
the clean handle of a wooden spoon. Cover and return to a boil.
Allow to boil 30 seconds. Stir in a circular motion and cover.
Turn heat to simmer and let cook 20 minutes. Fluff with fork
and serve sprinkled with onions. Serves 8–10.

Gougsou (Korean) Long, thin wheat flour noodle, used in hot and
cold soups and in stir fries with chile sauces. Japanese *somen*
are a good substitute.

Grape leaves (European, Middle Eastern, North African) Sold fresh
and brined to use as wrappings for rice mixtures, or as a platform
on which to grill meat. Rinse the extra salt off the brined ones, and
unless you have a chance to pick your own little tender ones you
will need to blanch them before stuffing. Most fillings include

ground meat, but I like the vegetarian ones better, such as Turk-ish *zaytinagly yaprk dolmasi,* with its minty rice and tomato filling.

RECIPE REFERENCE: Zaytinagly Yaprk Dolmasi, *The Arabian Delights Cookbook,* p. 58.

Guajillo chile, chile guaque, mirasól (Latin American, North African, Indian) A long reddish-brown or maroon smooth dried chile common to Mexican, Guatemalan, and South American cooking. It is also the base for the famous and delicious Tunisian hot sauce harissa. It is a fair substitute for the Indian Kashmiri chile, being definitely hot but not deadly.

Guava, feijoa, pineapple guava, apple guava, strawberry guava (Latin American, Caribbean, Asian) Guavas are small, round-to-oval fruits with thin smooth skin and pale flesh. The skin may vary from green to yellow to red or even almost black, but the fragrance, once experienced, is distinctive. The flesh is slightly grainy with a sort of pineapple/pear flavor. A ripe guava has a bit of give, but its skin does not yet show spots. Guavas are good alone, or with a bit of ham or as part of a fruit salad. Guava jam is common in the tropics, as is the thick guava paste *ate.* See also **Ate.**

⋞ H ⋟

Habañero pepper, caballero (Latin American) Widely reputed to be the hottest pepper grown (a Red Savina habañero tested out at 100 times hotter than a jalapeño) these little firebombs are especially popular in the Caribbean and in the Yucatán. They also appear fresh in salsas and pickled in pepper sauces. One use that gives an idea of their potency comes from the Yucatán. A raw habañero is shredded at the pointed end and stirred around in a sauce, then removed. In local terms, "the chile takes a walk through the sauce" and gives it a noticeable flavor. Habañeros are shorter and wider than jalapeños, looking more like a miniature bell pepper, and, like bells, come in green, yellow, red, orange, and the more exotic browns and purples. The name is Cuban, from Havana, but the fame is widespread. Flavor is not only hot but "lingering and perfumed," in the words of Mexican food writer Diana Kennedy. Some references will tell you they are not sold dried, but they are. They look like dried cherry tomatoes, a lighter, more orangy red than most dried chiles. Any small, ultrahot pepper makes a reasonable substitute, although you will miss that flowery flavor. Caribbean near-equivalents are the Haitian piment, the Jamaican Scotch bonnet, and the Trinidadian *chile congo*.

Hajikami su-zuké (Japanese) Young ginger, pickled whole in a sweet-and-sour syrup and used with fish sushi.

Hamed m'raked, pickled lemons (North African) Fermented, pickled lemons are used as both a cooking ingredient and a condiment in North African cuisines. The skin, which softens to a pulpy consistency, is the part used, giving a salty, tangy flavor, not much related to fresh lemon juice or lemon zest. They are sold in Arabic markets, or you can easily make your own. They can be kept up to a year, or even longer under refrigeration.

Harina para bollitos (Latin American) Cooked black-eyed peas, ground into flour and ready for the popular South American and Caribbean fritters, which are served as snacks and appetizers. Sometimes available in Latin American markets.

Harissa (North African, Middle Eastern) A hot chile pepper sauce with many variations that is a signature of North African cooking. The Tunisian version, my personal favorite, adds caraway seeds as well as garlic; Moroccan harissa skips the caraway, and Moroccan Jews often add vinegar to theirs. It is used to flavor couscous broth, as part of a marinade for olives, and as a spread for Algerian *karantika* bread, and I like it mixed with yogurt in baked potatoes. It is sold canned or in tubes in Middle Eastern markets. I haven't tried the tubes, but Mediterranean food specialist Paula Wolfert says they are not satisfactory. *Sambal ulek*, with cumin and/or caraway added, makes an acceptable substitute. One canned Tunisian label is Le Flambeau du Cap Bon. It contains red peppers, garlic, coriander, cumin, and salt. Or you can make your own. See also **Sambal ulek**.

RECIPE: Harissa

$1/2$ teaspoon cumin
$1/4$ teaspoon coriander seed
1 clove garlic, minced
1 red jalapeño, minced
$1/4$ cup chicken stock
1 tablespoon olive oil
1 teaspoon minced cilantro
$1/2$ teaspoon parsley
$1/8$ teaspoon cayenne
$1/4$ teaspoon salt

Toast cumin and coriander seed in a small dry skillet over medium heat for about 4 minutes. Purée with garlic, jalapeño, chicken stock, olive oil, cilantro, parsley, cayenne, and salt in blender or food processor. Makes $^1/_2$ cup.

Harusame, saifun (Japanese) Long thin noodles made of potato and cornstarch. They are used in soups and salads or deep-fried for a garnish.

Ha-shoga, ginger shoots (Japanese) Young ginger sprouts, served pickled as a complement to grilled fish and other dishes.

Hazelnut oil (European) A fragrant, luscious oil used for top-of-the-line vinaigrettes and for marinating fish and poultry, primarily in France. Mix with a light oil for sautéing, and try stirring a little into your best fettuccine instead of serving it *al burro.*

Hibiscus, sorrel, jamaica, rosella (Latin American). In Jamaica, this member of the hibiscus genus is called *sorrel,* although it isn't related botanically to sorrel. Probably the name was inspired by the similarity in flavor. In Mexico, it's called *jamaica* (pronounced *ha-MY-ca*) in honor of its origin. In both countries the dark red sepals from the blossoms are sold dried to make a tart, claret-colored brew which is served hot or cold, especially around Christmastime, often sugar sweetened and spiced with cinnamon and cloves. Rum is another popular addition. The seeds are used to make preserves, rather like rosehip preserves.

RECIPE: Jamaican Sorrel Tea

$1/4$ cup dried hibiscus flowers
3 cups sugar, or less according to taste
$2 1/2$ quarts boiling water

Steep hibiscus flowers and sugar in the hot water. Drain, cool, and serve. Serves 8 to 10.

———————————⋅⋚———————————

Hijiki, hair seaweed (Japanese, Chinese) Dry black strands that look like coarse hair. *Hijiki* is soaked before use (it expands a lot) and then sautéed, batter fried, or added to soups. Braising in a sweetened soy broth gives it a licoricelike flavor that is appreciated as a Japanese side dish. Like other sea vegetables, it's a good source of calcium for nondairy diets.

RECIPE REFERENCE: Hijiki No Ni Mono, *At Home with Japanese Cooking,* p. 131.

Hiyamugi (Japanese) Dried wheat noodles, about as long as spaghetti but slightly thicker, packaged in bunches and tied with a cloth ribbon. They are usually eaten cold, with garnishes and dipping sauce.

Hoisin sauce, Peking sauce, ten-flavored sauce, red vegetable sauce (Chinese) A thick sweetened soybean sauce with garlic and vinegar, not as hot as Sichuan sauce. Sold in supermarkets as well as Asian groceries, it is mixed with sesame oil or other ingredients to use as a dip for pork, and is also used for cooking meats and seafoods when a sweet rich glaze is wanted. Bottled hoisin sauce will keep indefinitely in its container. If it's in a metal jar you should switch it to a glass container after opening.

Hoja santa, hierba santa, tlanepa, momo, acuyo (Mexican) A sassafras-flavored herb, *Piper auritum sanctum,* used with fish and in tamales and green moles. It has a large, heart-shaped leaf, dark green on the surface and light green on its veined underside. The flower is long, very thin and stemlike, and creamy white. Use it fresh only.

Huitlacoche, cuitlacoche, corn smut (Mexican) Especially popular around Mexico City, this fabled fungus grows on corn, deforming the kernels into a grey-skinned mass, black and juicy inside. It sounds pretty ugly, and commercial corn growers have worked hard to keep it out of their fields, but I know friends who have had it once and go on yearning ever after, and some market growers now cultivate it deliberately. It is best fresh, after the rainy season, but you may find it frozen, which is preferable to canned, in some specialty markets.

RECIPE REFERENCE: **Huitlacoche con Calabacitas Estila Queretano,** *Recipes from the Regional Cooks of Mexico,* Diane Kennedy, p. 141.

Hungarian wax peppers (European) Long, shiny, handsome yellow peppers in two basic varieties, one sweet and the other (by European standards) hot. Often sold in a spicy vinegar pickle.

◦⌠ **I** ⌡◦

Indian pickled vegetables (Indian) Any Indian grocery will carry rows of bottled and canned pickles, often with a listing of completely unfamiliar ingredients. In our tiny town, the Sikh-run gas station has at least half a dozen varieties in its quick mart. These are not similar to the dry, salted pickled vegetables of China and Japan. They are a mixture of several vegetables and/or fruits, cut in substantial chunks and preserved in a strong brine, less sweet and less soft than a bottled chutney. Many have a strong taste of whole lemon or lime, or the sourness of green mango. They provide the flavor interest in a laborer's lunch of *naan* or rice and yogurt. It's hard to get much idea of the taste from the bottle label, and a little goes a long way for the uninitiated. As some Indian cookbooks strongly look down on the commercial products, it is worth trying a recipe on your own for comparison. (I always use organically grown lemons and limes for whole-fruit recipes, since not all the sprays used on the outside are intended for human consumption.)

RECIPE REFERENCE: Hot Lemon Pickle (Garam Nimboo Ka Achar), *Classic Indian Cooking,* p. 449.

Injera (African) The spongy, slightly sour bread that doubles as a serving utensil in Ethiopian restaurants, *injera* is a sort of giant sourdough crepe. It is cooked in thin rounds, large enough to hold an entire meal and drape over the platter. Traditionally made of ground, fermented teff, a tiny-seeded, protein-rich relative of millet that is an Ethiopian staple, it also comes in wheat versions. Many North American cooks, myself included, have had trouble making *injera* in the United States according to traditional recipes. Perhaps there is a difference in the teff available here or maybe the ambient yeasts that begin the fermenting process in Ethiopia are not found on this side of the Atlantic. Some recipes use wheat flour and club soda to approximate the correct flavor and texture, but I have not tried this shortcut. See also **Teff.**

◆§ J §◆

Jackfruit (Asian, Caribbean) A cousin of breadfruit, green and oval-shaped with a prickly rind, often weighing forty pounds or more. The juicy, sloppy, pale-yellow flesh can be eaten fresh as a fruit, avoiding the many seeds, and is also popular, unripe, as a vegetable. The seeds themselves are sometimes roasted and eaten like chestnuts, whose flavor they are purported to resemble. Perhaps I prepared them wrong, but I didn't like them. Both ripe and green jackfruit are available canned, which is a good thing because the fresh fruit's huge size makes it expensive and unwieldy, and its sticky juice clings tenaciously to hands and clothing. Unripe jackfruit is basic to the traditional Indonesian dish *gudeg,* in which it is combined with boiled eggs, coconut milk, and a paste of ground candlenut and shrimp. The ripe ones taste sort of like a pineapple custard.

Jalapeño chile (Latin American) The most familiar of Mexican hot chiles, jalapeños are dark green, sometimes mottled with black, with rounded shoulders and a pointed end. They are sold fresh and pickled, and are the standard for restaurant salsas. Jalapeños that are allowed to ripen and then smoked and dried are sold as chipotles, and their richer flavor is becoming increasingly popular. See also, **Chipotle.**

Jantaboon (Thai) Rice noodles, thicker and flatter than Chinese vermicelli. They need to be soaked and boiled.

Jasmine flower essence (Indian, Turkish) Similar to orange flower and rose water. It is used in Turkish compotes.

Jasmine rice (Thai) A long-grained, very fragrant rice that differs from basmati in its sweeter smell and slightly glutinous quality.

Jellyfish (Chinese) Sold dried, either whole or shredded. Soak overnight before using and then remove any red bits. Rinse in boiling water before using. Jellyfish strips can be stored for weeks, soaked and ready to use, by covering with water and changing the water daily. It is used in salads and other cold dishes, where its crunchy texture adds interest and its bland flavor does not compete.

Jerk seasoning (Caribbean) A Jamaican specialty, featuring scallions, hot peppers, and other spices (sometimes including juniper berries), varying with the cook. Used as a marinade for meats, especially chicken, goat, and fish, which you are then supposed to grill over a pimento-wood fire and serve with a lot of Red Stripe beer. For a less traditional but delicious version, mix with yogurt and use as a marinade for grilled chicken or an addition to roast potatoes. My husband recommends peanut butter and jerk sandwiches. I can't vouch for that, but I agree that jerk is versatile. It is available bottled in specialty food stores (we like the very hot variety from Walker's Wood), or you can make your own to taste.

RECIPE REFERENCE: Jerk Marinade, *Cold Weather Cooking,* by Sarah Leah Chase, p. 291

Jerusalem artichoke, girasole, topinambour, sunchoke (Mediterranean) No relation to artichokes but rather a perennial variety of sunflower. The Italian name, *girasole,* means "turns with the sun." The crisp, thin-skinned, lumpy tubers are good both cooked and raw, and sometimes are used as an addition to pasta dough. Jerusalem artichokes go particularly well with olive oil, and are used regularly in Turkish cooking, braised in a rich broth with or without other vegetables. They make good soup, either puréed or in chunks as part of a stew. Peeling is a chore and not really necessary unless the tubers are too lumpy to clean effectively. Larger ones will slip their peels after a 30-second blanching. Jchokes will discolor once cut, so either do them at the last minute or dip in acidulated water. The main advice is not to overcook them, as they turn quickly from a nice gentle crispness to an unappetizing mush.

Jicama, sah goh, yam bean, ahipa, bengjuang (Latin American, Chinese, Southeast Asian, Indonesian) The Chinese name means "sandy tuber," which is a reasonable description. The root of a morning-glory relative, jicama is shaped like a flattop onion but bigger, with tan skin and a crunchy, mildly sweet taste. It is native to Latin America but has traveled to Asia, where is it used like water chestnuts in stir fries and also boiled. It is most familiar to me as one of the street snacks of the Mexican Pacific coast, served in a paper cone with chunks of orange and a dash of lime juice and chile powder. For a slightly more complex version, try this.

———————— ❧ ————————

RECIPE: **Jicama Salad**

> 1 large jicama, peeled and sliced (about three cups)
> 3 medium oranges, peeled, seeded and cut into chunks
> 3 tablespoons sweet onion, chopped fine
> 3 tablespoons lime juice
> 1 cup roasted, unsalted peanuts
> 1 jalapeño, seeded and minced
> $^{1}/_{4}$ cup crumbled queso fresco
> salt to taste

Combine jicama, orange, and jalapeño in a serving bowl and mix in lime juice and salt. Grind peanuts into crumbs in a food processor, blender, or mortar and pestle. Sprinkle peanuts and cheese over salad and serve immediately. Serves 6 to 8.

———————— ❧ ————————

Jujubes, Chinese dates, red dates (Chinese, Korean) Used medicinally and in cooking and desserts. Jujubes are brownish-skinned, oblong fruit, up to two inches in diameter, with mealy pulp and a single pointed seed. They are more often sold dried, canned, or candied. Chinese cooks use these to provide some sweetness to slow-cooked chicken and fish and for sweets. Dried jujubes should be soaked half an hour in cold water before use in desserts. They can go into cooked dishes as is. Koreans value them for their medicinal properties, as exemplified in the rice dessert *yakshik* (*yak* means "medicine"). Figs or dates can be substituted.

ঙ্গ K ঌৎ

Kaffir lime, makrut, duan jeruk purut (Thai, Southeast Asian, Indonesian) The juice, rind, and leaves of *Citrus hystrix* are used for flavor and aroma. The rind is minced or pounded in curry pastes. The juice is used in sauces and salad dressings. The leaves are added to soups and curries and then removed before eating, like the bay leaf, whose flavor is somewhat similar. Fresh leaves are sometimes available in Asian markets. They have a heavenly aroma that the dried leaves can't match.

Kala namak, black salt (Indian) A naturally occurring salt that is brownish-black in its natural crystalline state and speckly pinkish-brown when powdered. Both forms are sold in Indian groceries. It is expensive for salt, but a little goes a long way. The smell is smoky with a distinct whiff of sulfur and the taste is distinctively tangy. It is used in Indian cooking as a condiment rather than as a seasoning.

RECIPE REFERENCE: **Aloo Chat,** *Classic Indian Cooking,* p. 105.

Kamaboko (Japanese) A mild, steamed sausage made of puréed, seasoned whitefish, which is sometimes dyed and formed into decorative shapes. The most common form is a white log with an outer layer of bright pink. The taste is mild. It may be eaten plain with a dipping sauce and is often added to soups. Sometimes it is served layered with slices of various seafood as a sort of marine parfait. *Kamaboko* will keep, refrigerated, for three or four days.

Kanpyo (Japanese) Long, dried gourd strips used as an edible string to tie up food packages such as nori wrappings and for decorations on sushi. It should be white, uniform, and sweet smelling. Rinse it in water, rub with salt, and soak in lukewarm water 15 minutes; then boil until soft. Dried *kanpyo* will keep indefinitely in an airtight container.

Kapee (Pan-Asian) A variant on Thai shrimp sauce, made by combining shrimp and salt and leaving the mixture to dry in the sun. It also can be made with squid.

Katsuobushi (Japanese) Dried bonito, used to make the essential Japanese stock, dashi, and also as a garnish for vegetables. It comes in all degrees of preparation, from woodlike blocks to bags of fine flakes or shavings, called *hanagatsuo* or *kezuribushi*. The blocks require a special shaver. It is also popular mixed with a little soy sauce as a filling for *omusubi* (rice sandwiches), popular Japanese picnic fare. Japanese stores sell single-portion packs of *katsuobushi,* or you can get about $^1/_4$ pound and make gallons of dashi.

Kebsa spices (North African, Middle Eastern) A traditional Saudi and Gulf spice mixture of at least cardamom, cinnamon, cumin, and red or black pepper. One recipe calls for 1 tablespoon red pepper, $1^1/_2$ teaspoons cumin, $1^1/_2$ teaspoons cinnamon, 1 teaspoon cloves, 1 teaspoon black pepper, 1 teaspoon ground cardamom, 1 teaspoon nutmeg, 1 teaspoon ground coriander, 1 teaspoon ground *loomi* (dried limes or lemons). Much used in the eponymous *kebsa* dishes, which are Saudi Arabia's answer to paella.

RECIPE REFERENCE: Saudi Fish Soup (Shorbat al Samak) *The Arabian Delights Cookbook,* p. 103.

Kecap manis (Pan-Asian) A thick soy sauce, sweetened with molasses, used in Java, where it comes in spiced and plain versions. *Kecap,* pronounced "ketchup," is the Javanese word for soy sauce and also the source of the English name for a thick, sweetened sauce. Can be substituted for the "dark sweet soy" called for in some Chinese recipes. See also **Sambal kecap** and **Soy sauce.**

Kewra (South Asian) A floral-smelling leaf related to *rampa* or screwpine, it is sold as an essence, often right next to the *rampa* and the rose water in Indian groceries.

Kimchee, kimchi (Korean, Japanese) Sauerkraut with attitude, kimchee is one of my favorite condiments as well as being a personal litmus test for people's willingness to experiment with unfamiliar food, since it looks funny, smells strong, and tastes wonderful. The most familiar variety in North American markets is made with nappa cabbage, green onions, chiles, and garlic. Strongly flavored and well fermented, this is a winter kimchee. Summer varieties may be simply briefly salted, rather than fermented. Cucumber is one popular ingredient. Turnips, daikon, and greens such as sweet potato vines, sold in fat braids in Korean markets, also can go into kimchee, along with meats and seafood. If you make your own, which isn't hard, you can eventually create your own variations.

Ki no mé (Japanese) Small leaf of the prickly ash tree, sometimes found fresh in Asian markets. Like its better-known berry (used to make *Sansho* or Sichuan pepper), it has a captivating aroma and a sharp but not overpowering bite. Bruise the leaves before serving, and then chop or use whole in salads or soups.

Kinugoshi (Japanese) A silken or soft tofu, as compared with the firmer variety more used in Chinese cooking. It is made from yellow soybeans. Sometimes it is deep-fried and then recooked, which gives it an open, spongy texture and makes it a better ab-sorber for other flavors.

Kishk (Arabic) One of the world's oldest and most ingenious foods, a tangy and nutritious mixture of yogurt and bulgur wheat, be-lieved to have been discovered in the Fertile Crescent and used for millennia by desert nomads. It looks like very fine ground cornmeal and keeps pretty much forever. It is sold for high prices in Middle Eastern specialty stores. Or, with patience (and a hot climate) you can make your own.

RECIPE REFERENCE: **Kick Ma Bad,** *From the Land of Figs and Olives. Makes a lifetime supply, unless you are Bedouin.*

Knafa, knafeh, konafa, kadaifa, katafi (Middle Eastern, Euro-pean) A soft, uncooked wheat dough, looking rather like shred-ded wheat, used in making pastries. It is sold frozen in Middle Eastern and Greek stores. Shredded Filo dough can be substi-tuted.

RECIPE REFERENCE: **Knafeh bil jibneh,** *The Arabian Delights Cookbook.*

Kochujang (Korean) A spicy condiment made with soy bean paste, ground red pepper, and glutinous rice flour. One of the essential seasonings of the Korean kitchen, it is used in stews, vegetable dressings and dips to help give the rich flavors characteristic of Korean food. Sold bottled in well-stocked Korean groceries, or you can substitute Chinese chile paste with garlic.

Konbu, tasima, dried kelp (Japanese, Korean) Dried sheets of the prodigious seaweed bullwhip kelp, which is green/brown and rubbery when fresh and stiff and grey-green when dried, with a powdery finish of precipitated salt. *Konbu* tenderizes the ingredients it is cooked with and adds a slight sweetness in addition to its marine flavor. It is used most famously to make the Japanese fish stock dashi. An ounce of dried kelp makes four servings of dashi. After the stock is cooked, you can remove the *konbu* and use it as an edible wrapper for rice or vegetables. The best Japanese *konbu* is supposed to be from Hokkaido. Domestic kelp is also available in some U.S. natural foods stores. Its harvest and preparation has become a cottage industry in the San Juan Islands of Washington State. Wipe gently rather than rinsing before use. Strips can be braided and deep-fried to make culinary baskets. Fresh kelp is sold in Korea as a soup ingredient, and I have eaten it in the U.S. as part of a divine vegetable chowder.

Konnyaku (Japanese) A translucent, jellylike block made from devil's tongue root. It is sold in rectangles sitting in water, like a small, gold-brown tofu, labeled yam paste or alimentary paste. Like tofu, its main role is to absorb other flavors and provide a texture contrast with crisp vegetables. It has a slightly unpleasant odor when fresh, but this disappears after blanching. Keep it refrigerated in water, like tofu.

RECIPE REFERENCE: **Vegetables and Seasoned Rice (Kayaku Gohan)**, *At Home with Japanese Cooking,* pp. 73–74.

Krachai, rhizome, lesser ginger (Southeast Asian) The ingredient listed as *rhizome* in Thai curry paste, it is also served raw as a fresh vegetable. It's a cousin of ginger (*Kaempferia pandurata*) and looks like a smaller, thinner version with fingerlike roots. It can be used interchangeably with galangal. Sometimes it is found fresh in Asian markets, more often shredded and dried, labeled "rhizome."

Krupuk udang, prawn crackers (Indonesian, Chinese) Popular, puffy crackers flavored with shrimp or prawn. The best-known are the small pastel ones served in Chinese restaurants, but some Asian groceries will sell more flavorful Indonesian varieties, dried but not cooked, that you can fry up at home. The taste varies with the kind of flour used—wheat, rice, cassava, or corn, and the amount of seafood flavoring. Uncooked *krupuk* will keep indefinitely; cooked ones need to be stored in an airtight container.

Kudzu, fun got (Chinese, Japanese) The starch and the root it comes from are both sold in Asian groceries for use as thickeners in soups and sauces.

⋖ L ⋗

Labana (North African, Middle Eastern) A cheeselike paste derived from yogurt (*laban*), when most of the water has been extracted. Available from Middle Eastern stores. It can be approximated by blending together dry cottage cheese or farmer's cheese with a little yogurt and a tablespoon of oil, or by hanging your own whole-milk yogurt to drain through cheesecloth overnight. *Labana* is used in dips and soups, and is mixed with olive oil and lemon juice to dress salads containing strong-tasting greens. Mixed with milk and water and then poured into sautéed garlic and onion, it makes a savory liquid in which to poach eggs, the result being served as a soup. See also **Kishk.**

Laksa noodles (Southeast Asian) Thick rice vermicelli used in soups and curries with coconut milk sauces in Malaysia, Singapore, and Indonesia.

Largo chile (Latin American) A hot yellow pepper, sometimes sold canned. It is an acceptable substitute for the South American highlands favorite *ají amarillo,* which can be hard to come by.

Leblebi (Turkish) Chickpeas sold as snacks or street food. The white ones are partially cooked and then dried; yellow ones are partially cooked and then roasted. I like the yellow ones better. See also **Garbanzo beans.**

Lemongrass, sarai sari (Pan-Asian, Thai, Malaysian) One of the foundation flavors of Southeast Asian cooking, and a revelation to first-time samplers of Thai food. It is sold powdered or as dry flakes, but generally is also available fresh, usually in a bucket of water, in Asian markets. Fresh lemongrass looks rather like a bunch of long, stiff scallions. The taste is tangy without being sour, wonderfully refreshing, and the perfect complement to fish sauces and shrimp cakes. To use fresh lemongrass, remove the stiff, pale outer leaves and make thin slices across the stem from the base to where leaves begin to separate. Mince or pound the slices to release the flavor and scent. Dried flakes should be ground before adding to other pastes. Dried stalks should be soaked half an hour before use. Iced tea is made from dried lemongrass flakes. The pounded ends of the leaves are used as a brush for basting and barbecue. I have read that lemongrass is easy to grow as a houseplant if you can buy a bunch with a bit of root remaining, but I haven't tried it.

Lobhia, black-eyed peas (Indian) The American Southern favorite also is popular in India, where its relatively quick cooking time makes it useful for dal.

Longan, dragon eyes, loan ngon (Chinese) I love these. They look sort of like a bunch of very round, yellow grapes and have a mild, refreshing flavor and a big shiny seed that's fun to play with. They are used as a garnish and a soup flavoring in Chinese cooking, but I prefer to eat them fresh out of hand, as do my Hong Kong friends who introduced me to them. They are generally available canned and sometimes fresh in Chinese groceries.

Lontong (Indonesian) Compressed rice, either long or short grain, cooked in a tight packet of banana leaf or a cloth bag so that the grains mass together into a solid lump. *Lontong* is traditionally eaten cold with a contrastingly hot sauce. Sometimes you can find rice sold already in a bag and ready to cook.

Loomi, leimoon basra, leimoon aswad, leimoon omani (Middle Eastern) Dried limes or lemons produced in Iraq, Iran, and Oman. Brown, hard, and light as a Ping-Pong ball, they are sold whole and powdered in Arabic markets. Iranians use them when cooking rice and other dishes to produce a sharp, tart flavor. Wash, halve, and remove the seeds, then simmer with other ingredients in stews and rice dishes. Or you can pierce the loomi and let the flavor percolate through. Start with one loomi for 4 servings. Ground loomi is added to lentil dip.

> RECIPE REFERENCE: **Stuffed Fish with Sun Dried Lime** (**Semak ma Loomi**), *From the Gulf states. The Arabian Delights Cookbook,* p. 212.

Loquat, Japanese medlar, akidinya (Chinese, Japanese) These fruits are distantly related to apples and pears. They have a sweet, seedy pulp, cream to orange in color. Loquats can be used in pear or plum recipes or eaten fresh.

Lotus leaves (Chinese, Southeast Asian) Fan-shaped leaves, sold dried in packages and used to wrap *dim sum,* to which they give a distinctive, slightly sweet flavor. Fresh young leaves can be eaten raw; soak dried leaves at least an hour before using as a wrapping.

> RECIPE REFERENCE: **Stuffed Lotus Leaves (Lin Bau Nor Main Fon),** *From the Earth: Chinese Vegetarian Cooking,* pp. 144–145.

Lotus root, leen ngau, renkon, hasu, bhain (Chinese, Japanese, Indian, Vietnamese) An odd looking, wasp-waisted root, pale tannish in color, fresh *Nelumbo nucifera* looks rather like a percussion instrument in an ethnic band. When the root is cut crosswise, a series of holes make a sort of snowflake pattern. Commonly sold fresh in Asian markets, it should be firm and unblemished. Fresh lotus root is sometimes stuffed with glutinous rice for a sweet dish, used like potatoes in soups and stews, or sliced and deep-fried, with or without tempura batter. To use fresh, peel like a potato and cut crosswise or on the diagonal; it will discolor once cut, so put in acidulated water if appearance is important. Lotus root is also sold canned, plain and pickled, in Asian markets, used in Indian chutneys, and boiled and mashed to go into dal. Don't overcook or it gets unpleasantly mealy. The seeds, which represent fertility and birth to Chinese households, are puréed and used to make confections or incorporated into pastries. A sweet-and-sour lotus root pickle, though available canned, is easy to make at home.

————————— ❧ —————————

RECIPE: Sweet and Sour Lotus Root

>1 small fresh lotus root (about 1 foot long)
>2 cups cold water
>3 tablespoons rice vinegar
>**Sweet-and-Sour Sauce:**
>$1/2$ cup rice vinegar
>$1/4$ cup sugar
>$1/4$ teaspoon salt

Make the sweet-and-sour sauce by heating all ingredients over low heat until the sugar dissolves. Stir and then let cool. Peel lotus root and cut into thin rounds. Soak in acidulated water for 10 minutes. Rinse. Combine water and rice vinegar in a stainless steel pan, bring to a boil, and cook the root for 2–3 minutes (it should still be crisp). Drain and marinate in sweet-and-sour sauce at least 2 hours. Keep refrigerated and replenish marinade if necessary. It will keep for months as long as the slices are submerged. Makes about 30 slices.

Lumpia (Philippine) The name refers to both the Philippine version of spring rolls and the wrapper—a transparent pastry made of wheat flour, cornstarch, and eggs—used to contain them. Both the rolls and the wrappers are often sold at Philippine groceries.

Lychee (Chinese) The dried fruits (called *lychee nuts*) are the most familiar, but the fresh ones are sometimes available and are prized both for eating out of hand and for cooking with pork, where their delicate sweetness complements the rich meat. Lychees also are sold canned in syrup in Asian markets and sometimes in supermarkets. Dried lychees have thin, brownish shells and dark prunelike flesh. Fresh ones are red on the outside and pale and translucent on the inside, with a large pit. Look for them in the summer in well-stocked Chinese markets.

⊰ M ⊱

Macapuno, kopyor, coconut sport, mutant gelatinous coconut (Philippine, Indonesian) A coconut mutation in which the flesh does not harden as the nut matures, but stays soft and mushy and mixes naturally with the coconut water. It is popular in Indonesia for making ice cream and is sold in groceries serving Philippine communities, preserved in syrup, alone or with other fruits and sweetened black beans, for use in desserts.

Mahlepi, mahleb (Middle Eastern, European, Turkish) The seed of a small wild black cherry (*Prunus mahleb*), which is sold whole, chopped, or ground fine in Arab markets and is also used in Greek baking. The whole seeds are small and tan, shaped rather like tiny lemon seeds. The best flavor—subtle and fruity, sometimes described as peach-like—comes from the freshly ground whole seeds. *Mahleb* is used to flavor breads, cookies, and sweet pastries. To experiment, add about 1/2 to 1 teaspoon of *mahleb* for 2 cups of flour. For best storage, buy it whole and keep it in the freezer if not using it immediately.

RECIPE REFERENCE: **Aromatic Festive Bread (Madnakash, Shooshma Hatz)** (Syria and Armenia), *Flatbreads and Flavors,* pp. 235–236.

Maldive fish, umbalakada (Pan-Asian) Dried salted tuna from the Maldive Islands, used dried and powdered or chopped in Sri Lankan and Indian vegetable curries. It is sold in Indian markets. Dried cod or shrimp or katsuobushi flakes can be substituted.

Malunggay, horseradish tree, malongai, reseda, shajmah (Asian, West African) A versatile plant (*Moringa pterygosperma*) little known in North America, although the leaves are sold, occasionally fresh but usually frozen, in many Asian markets. The leaves are large, with many leaflets. They are cooked like spinach—boiled, steamed, or stir-fried. The young flowers and fruits are also cooked as a vegetable, and the roots, which have a peppery, horseradishlike taste, are grated as a condiment.

Mamey, mammee, St. Domingo apricot (Caribbean, Mexican) A native of the Caribbean, this apple-sized fruit has a light-brown, rough, shell-like skin. The pink/orange flesh is smooth and sweet with a delicate almondlike flavor when fully ripe. Once the inside has patches of brown, flavor is failing. It is eaten both raw and cooked, with the tarter, less ripe fruits used in jams and jellies. Eau de Creole, a Caribbean liqueur, is distilled from the flowers. (*Mammee sapote*, popular in Cuba, is a different fruit.)

Mango, mangue, mon go (Indian, Pan-Asian, Latin American, African) A completely wonderful and luscious fruit, which needs nothing but a squeeze of lime to make it perfect. Mango milkshakes, sorbets, custards, and other desserts are delectable but superfluous in my view. Like papaya and pineapple, mango will never be at its best on a North American supermarket shelf, as it does not travel well when fully ripe. In countries where mangos abound, the unripe fruits are used in salads, chutneys, and pickles, or chopped fine for the slight sourness they add to a seasoning. Raw mango "cheeks" are sun dried and powdered to make brownish-green *amchoor,* a souring agent for curries. See also **Amchoor.**

Mangosteen (Southeast Asian) This is a striking fruit with a magnificent reputation. The shell is round and dark, rather like a flattened plum, with a bright red inner shell and lobed white flesh. Inside it looks rather like a head of peeled garlic. It has a melting texture and sweet taste. It is best fresh, but hard to find. You can buy it canned in well-stocked Asian markets.

Manisan pala (Indonesian, Caribbean) Candied fruit of the nutmeg tree, of which nutmeg is the seed and mace is the seed coating. The fruit, which looks like a small, pale peach, is also used on some Caribbean islands to make liqueur.

Masa (Latin American) Ground dried corn, with lime added, is the foundation of tortillas and therefore of much of Mexican and Central American cuisine. A really good corn tortilla is as different from the tough, bitter, overpreserved supermarket variety as garden *petit pois* from canned peas, and the smell is the most evocative fragrance I know, bringing back in a rush my happy months in Mexico. Masa is widely available in supermarkets (the Quaker Oats brand is fine) and can sometimes be bought fresh or frozen at Latin American markets. If you can get it fresh, freeze what you don't use right away, as it sours quickly. It also is used to make tamales. See also **Arepas.**

Masala (Indian) The word means a spice mixture, generally dry, but sometimes is also applied to pastes of ground herbs and spices. Commercial curry powder is one kind of masala, but with too much reliance on turmeric and mustard to much resemble any authentic regional mixture. Masalas generally are added at or near the end of cooking, because wet heat changes the characteristics of some of the flavors. There are nearly as many masalas as there are Indian cooks, and any Indian grocery will have rows of little cardboard containers of ready-mixed spices earmarked for different dishes. The store-bought powders I have tried have not been very good, though, so it is worth it to prepare at least a couple of the basics on your own. Whatever kind you use, store it in an airtight container. *Garam masala* is the most familiar combination of flavors. Its basic proportions are $1/4$ cup green cardamom pods, one 3-inch cinnamon stick, $1/2$ tablespoon whole cloves, and $1/2$ tablespoon black peppercorns. At its simplest it is the basic spicing mixture of classic Moghul cuisine, which is known for its subtlety rather than its firepower. After shelling the cardamoms, you first crush and then grind the spices to about $1/3$ cup of powder, which will obviously bear no relation to grocery-store curry powder. The kind of *garam masala* more familiar to restaurant goers—because it is the one popular in North India, where most Indian restaurant recipes originate—adds about 2 tablespoons each of cumin and coriander seeds to the mixture, giving it a warmth of flavor. (See specific names for other masala mixtures.)

Masoor dal, masar dal (Indian) The fastest cooking of the dals, this lentil has a brown skin when whole but is generally sold split and skinned, a clear pinkish orange that becomes yellow in cooking. It cooks quickly and makes a thin, light purée. It is often cooked very simply, with a little turmeric and some garlic-flavored butter.

Mastic, sakiz (Turkish, Indian) Resin from a small evergreen acacia tree, *Pistacia lentiscus*. It is used like chewing gum and is also used for flavor and taste in sweet breads, milk puddings, and ice cream. Mastic is available in chunks of varying sizes in Middle Eastern and Indian markets.

Matsutake (Japanese) A largish firm-fleshed mushroom (*Armillaria ponderosa*) that has a wide, flat top and pale flesh. It is sold fresh in some supermarkets and Japanese groceries. At least the first time, simply marinate and grill it to get the unadulterated flavor.

RECIPE: **Broiled matsutake**
Wild Mushroom Recipes, by Puget Sound Mycological Society, p. 40.

> 5 small *matsutakes*
> 2 tablespoons *mirin*
> 1 1/2 tablespoons Japanese soy sauce

Slice mushrooms lengthwise into three pieces. Marinate an hour in *mirin* and soy sauce. Grill until tender, basting once or twice. Serves 2 or 3.

Mazapan (Latin American) Latin American cooks took the Spanish ground almond sweet marzipan (which came to Spain with the

Arabs) and adapted it to indigenous ingredients—peanuts or squash seeds. A Yucatecan version is made with pumpkin seeds; a peanut mazapan is sold in little disks in Mexican markets and many supermarkets. See also **Pepitas.**

Melitazanaki glyko (Greek) Small eggplants, stuffed with almonds and preserved in sweet syrup. The effect is more of like a candy than like a vegetable, using the eggplant's spongy texture to soak up lots of sugar. A Greek student I met years ago in Seattle received regular care packages of these from his mother as a cure for homesickness.

Menudo (Mexican) Soup made from tripe, hominy, pork, and chile, traditionally served with condiments of chopped onion, lime wedges, and oregano. Beloved in Michoacan, the state where many of the Mexican immigrants to the United States come from, and therefore more widely available in the United States than you might expect for a dish featuring innards. In my opinion it's the ultimate comfort food—both flavorful and soothing. Sold canned in Mexican groceries and in many supermarkets.

Merguez (North African, Middle Eastern) A popular Algerian sausage, made with lamb or beef and spiced with garlic, salt, pepper, cumin, coriander, sumac, chile, and paprika, and stuffed in casings. An Algerian Jewish version adds caraway and leaves out the sumac.

Mesclun, mesticanza (Italian, French) A Provençal salad mixture of various greens, eaten alone or mixed with lettuce. Farmers' markets and specialty groceries now sell it for many dollars a pound. Some common additions are radicchio, arugula, *mache*, chicory, endive, peppergrass, and dandelion greens.

Mirin (Japanese) A sweet rice wine used exclusively for cooking. It adds sweet flavor and a shiny glaze to marinades and boiled or grilled dishes. Flavor-added varieties also are available.

Miso, tauco (Japanese, Indonesian, Chinese) A nutrient-rich paste made by grinding and fermenting a mixture of steamed rice, cooked soybeans, and salt. Varieties of miso have different colors and flavors, influenced by the type and proportion of rice. There are three basic categories in descending order of pungency: *Aka, chu,* and *shiro. Aka miso* is made with white rice, is reddish brown and salty sweet, and is the base for many miso soups and marinades. *Chu,* often sold as *shinshu,* is milder in taste and golden brown in color. *Shiro* is called "white miso" but is actually a pale tan. It has more rice than soy and a slightly sweet flavor. It's popular in pickles and meat toppings. *Genmai miso,* made with brown rice, is golden in color, has a grainier texture, and is used mostly for sauces and spreads. *Mugi miso* is made with barley. Miso is sold in tubs in Japanese and natural foods stores. It will keep refrigerated basically forever.

Mochi, ddok rice cakes (Japanese, Korean, Indonesian) These versatile treats are not to be confused with the puffed rice cakes common in natural foods stores and more recently moved into supermarkets. In fact they are on the other side of the spectrum—dense, soft, and satiny rather than crisp and airy. The most refined version is Japanese *omochi,* the sweetened, gently colored, and exquisitely decorated pastries, often filled with sweet bean paste, used in the tea ceremony and sold in Japanese groceries. Plain fresh *mochi* are also grilled or boiled and added to soups, skewered for kabobs, or wrapped with nori for a snack. Fresh unsweetened *mochi* may be available at Japanese groceries and electric mochi-makers are sold in some shops. Shrink-wrapped brown rice *mochi,* flavored in variations from sweet to savory, is sold in the refrigerator section of many natural foods stores. It has its virtues, but the satiny, refined quality and subtle taste of the traditional type are not among them.

Mole (Latin American) *Mole* is a generic term referring to a smooth sauce containing peppers. Versions of it predate the European conquest of Mexico. The best known is *mole poblano,* or country sauce, an inspired mixture of bitter chocolate, chiles, spices, and nuts, served on chicken or turkey. The Aztec leader Moctezuma is supposed to have served it to Cortés, thus introducing Europeans to chocolate. It's fun to make *mole poblano* from scratch, at least once. After that, you may want to do as most Mexican cooks do and buy prepared versions, either a thick paste in a jar or a small can of powder, which has enough firepower to handle a good-sized turkey. In either case, dilute the mixture with chicken broth and follow your recipe's directions. There are many other moles in Mexican cooking. Oaxaca alone (a culinary paradise) has seven famous ones. Moles often use ground pumpkin or other seeds for thickening, giving them a characteristic smooth richness that goes wonderfully with the spices and peppers.

Molokhia, mlookheeyeh, Spanish sorrel, Spanish okra, Spanish jute, Jew's mallow (North African, Indian) A leafy plant resembling spinach or chard that is said to have been the favorite food of the ancient Egyptians. It is available fresh and dried, brined, or frozen in Middle Eastern markets, and is also used in North Africa and Syria. Food historian Copeland Marks has also seen the stir-fried fresh leaves in Calcutta. It's slightly glutinous, like okra, but bland and a bit astringent. *Molokhia* is also used in a vegetable stew with root vegetables, summer squash, tomato, and onion, flavored with cumin, allspice, garlic, and cilantro. Two ounces dried are equivalent to one pound fresh and will flavor a quart of soup. Soak the dried leaves 20 minutes in warm water with a little lemon juice.

RECIPE REFERENCE: **Chicken Molokhia Palestinian Style,** *From the Land of Figs and Olives,* p. 141.

Mugi cha, poricha, barley tea (Japanese, Korean) A hot-weather drink made from roasted barley. Packets of the prepared barley are sold in the tea section of Japanese groceries. To make, add one cup of *mugi cha* to 2 quarts water. Reduce heat and let simmer a few minutes, then strain through a colander and serve over ice. Koreans drink it hot or cold.

Mugwort (Japanese) A potherb sold dried in Japanese stores and natural foods stores, where it is valued as part of a macrobiotic diet. It is used to make tea and is sometimes added to soups.

Muligapuri (Indian) A condiment mix of fenugreek seeds and roasted powdered red chile and spices, eaten with skillet breads such as *idlis* and *dosas*. See also **Fenugreek.**

Mung beans, moong dal, validal green gram bean, mongo, dau xanh (Chinese, Indian, Japanese, Philippine, Vietnamese) Little round dried beans sold in any number of formats—whole and green (or more rarely black or brown), peeled and yellow, split, oiled or not. Also the source of standard bean sprouts, available fresh and canned and also easy to do at home. Koreans make a variety of tofu, called *chongpo muk,* out of mung bean flour, and a popular fritter, *pindatto,* also known as "Korean pizza," from the ground beans themselves. The ubiquitous bean thread noodles are made from mung bean starch, and Indian cooks use mung bean flour for breads and sweets as well as cooking the whole or split beans for dal. The split bean is what is known as *moong dal* in India; the whole ones are called *sabat moong.* Mung beans are relatively easy to digest, as beans go, and are cooked with rice and served to invalids in India.

Mussels, hak hin, cozze, muscoli, pecei (Chinese, Japanese, European) A small, black-shelled mollusk (the Chinese name means "black clam") that is one of the easiest to prepare and most delicious seafoods. It is one of the animal foods permitted to vegetarian Buddhists, along with clams and oysters, so it has a particular importance in East Asian cuisine. It is also much more popular in Europe than in the Americas; I once ate in a Belgian restaurant where every entrée featured mussels. Growing up on Puget Sound, I have always had fresh mussels free for the taking—my preteen daughter, who otherwise prefers to live on corn dogs and pizza, will personally gather, clean, cook, and devour a bowl of *moules marinière*—so it was news to me that some Asian markets sell mussels dried, which concentrates their flavor but also makes them tough. Reconstitute in warm water before using.

RECIPE REFERENCE: **Mussel and Noodle Soup,** *From the Earth: Chinese Vegetarian Cooking,* p. 226.

Mustard green, preserved (Chinese) This versatile condiment is pickled with salt, water, sugar, and vinegar, and is sold canned or in crocks. It is sometimes labeled with the common names of the various varieties of mustard, such as Green-in-Snow and Red-in-Snow.

Mustard oil (Indian) Cooking oil infused with mustard flavor (and smell), popular in Bengali and Kashmiri cooking. Plain oil can be substituted, with mustard seeds cooked in it.

✑ N ✑

Naeng myun (Korean) Thin, long, brown noodles made from buckwheat flour and potato starch or cornstarch. They are usually served cold in broth with garnishes. These are quite chewy, so much so that a recent traveler to Korea reported that table servers routinely carry scissors to help customers get their dinners into manageable pieces.

Naméko (Japanese, Chinese) Round orange mushrooms with a slippery coating, sold canned in Asian markets. They have a rich flavor, stronger than straw mushrooms, and are good in miso soups. They should be used within a few days after opening.

Naseberry, sapodilla (Caribbean, Latin American) A fruit native to Central America and the Caribbean. It grows on a tree with bay-like leaves, whose sap is the raw material for chewing gum. The fruit is round, about four inches in diameter, somewhat reminiscent of a bigger, smoother kiwi. The pulp has shiny, small black seeds and is translucent, apricot colored, fragrant, and very sweet. It's eaten fresh and used to make custard and ice cream. Naseberries are soft and spoil quickly, so wide distribution is unlikely, but it's worth looking for. The trees are big, and the market lady told me you have to climb them to harvest, as the fruit is too soft to drop without damage.

Natto (Japanese) A pressed cake of fermented soybeans with a rank smell and a strong, somewhat mustardy flavor, made by inoculating cooked soybeans with a cultivated bacterium. The beans are still whole, but coated with a stringy slime; hence the colloquial name "bean snot." Natto is used as a topping for rice or noodles or in miso soups. It is very nutritious—high in protein and fiber; low in fat—but not very attractive or, to me, tasty.

Nigella, kalonji (Indian, Middle Eastern) Small, pointy black seeds of a close cousin of the stalwart cottage garden plant "love in a mist." Dried seeds are used whole and ground, giving an aromatic, oniony flavor, and are used on breads, in chutneys, in *raitas*, in salads, and on vegetables. The seeds are sold in Indian and Middle Eastern markets. In Indian cooking, they are added to oil at the beginning of cooking, as with mustard seeds and fenugreek, and cooked until sizzling before other ingredients are added. They can be sprinkled on steamed vegetables (try them with green beans) or mixed with sesame on breads.

Nitter kibbeh (Ethiopian) A golden yellow clarified butter flavored with aromatic spices. This is the secret to some of the transfor-

mative miracles of Ethiopian cooking, where collards and cottage cheese develop a complex and satisfying flavor. It's also
great to melt a just little onto your boiled new potatoes. I have
never seen it for sale, although I expect it must be available in
some African markets. It's easy though a bit time-consuming to
make, and you could streamline the process by buying ghee,
melting it, and letting the spices steep overnight and then
straining it according to the process below. (To make plain ghee,
follow the directions below without the spices.) See also **Ghee.**

———————— ✎ ————————

RECIPE: **Nitter Kibbeh**
Winter Harvest, p. 218.

> 1 pound unsalted butter
> 4 tablespoons onion, chopped
> 1 $^1/_2$ tablespoons garlic, minced
> 2 teaspoons fresh ginger, grated
> $^1/_2$ teaspoon ground turmeric
> 2 whole green cardamom seeds or $^1/_2$ teaspoon ground
>   cardamom
> one 1-inch stick cinnamon
> 2 or 3 whole cloves
> $^1/_8$ teaspoon ground nutmeg

Slowly melt butter in a saucepan and then bring it to a boil.
When butter is covered with foam, add all remaining ingredients. Lower heat, and simmer, uncovered, over very low heat
until the surface is transparent and the milk solids are on the

bottom. This can take up to an hour. Pour off the clear liquid (leaving as much residue as possible in the pan) and strain through a double layer of damp cheesecloth. Strain twice more if you expect to keep the *nitter kibbeh* for more than a few weeks. After three strainings, it should keep for several months at room temperature and indefinitely under refrigeration. Makes about 2 cups.

Nixtamal (Latin American) Dried corn kernels that have been cooked in a solution of lime and water. Basically, this is hominy. It is the last step before grinding into masa for tortillas, but is also used on its own.

Noodles For those of us who grew up on spaghetti with red sauce, the variety and importance of noodles is a continuing astonishment. Long-keeping, quick-cooking and versatile, they have penetrated nearly every cereal-based culture, which is most of them. My first epiphany was when I studied in Italy and first tasted fresh pasta in a fraction of its infinite variety. Next came the revelations of Asian noodles, thick and thin, hot and cold, and all delicious. As with chiles, noodle selection for the novice is complicated by the fact that they are sold fresh and dried, and that the same basic combination of ingredients may have picked up several common names as it moved from culture to culture.

Italian pastas By Italian law, these are made of semolina, the flour made from the hardest part of hard durum wheat. That explains their yellow color, and also the extreme brittleness of the dried pasta and its ability to hold all sorts of fanciful shapes: mostaccioli, farfalle, ziti, fusilli, and the like. They require longer cooking than most Asian noodles. Italian pastas are more likely than their Asian counterparts to be covered with a smooth sauce rather than a lightly cooked assortment of ingredients, so they are cooked to retain a bit of tooth. Italian pasta may have eggs added (once again, the government monitors the correct proportion) as well as additional ingredients such as spinach, tomatoes, or chestnuts. Even our local, solidly plebeian grocery now carries fancy pasta blends—lemon pepper fettuccine and the like—and of course the fresh is worth buying or making at least once, to realize how good flour and water can be.

Asian wheat noodles These are made with soft wheat, which has much more accessible starch grains and gives a markedly different color and texture. They tend to be soft and slippery. The best known in North America is the ubiquitous ramen egg noodle, which is generally fried before going into those little soup packets, but which also is available plain and fresh in Asian markets. Japanese *udon*, which are bigger and thicker, are in the same general category.

Rice noodles The best-known kind are the little rice sticks or rice vermicelli, thin as string and dried into little coiled nests. They are soaked for use in Vietnamese *pho* and other soups, or deep-fried into a dramatic puffy white mass that serves as the base of a chicken or seafood salad. Other rice noodles may be thicker, like *jantaboon*, or the Philippine *pancit luglug* and Indonesian *laksa*. Fresh rice noodles are sometimes available in Chinese markets. They are sold in wide sheets or cut into ³/4-inch strips. Soft, smooth, flimsy, and very bland, they absorb other flavors well.

Buckwheat Japanese buckwheat *soba* is the best known, but *naeng myun* and thinner *dang myun* are Korean staples. The hearty, chewy buckwheat is often mixed with flavoring ingredients ranging from green tea to sweet potatoes. *Sobas* are eaten cold in the summer with a dipping sauce, or hot in a spicy broth.

Vegetable-based noodles Mung bean starch is the main source, making the ubiquitous bean threads and Philippine *pancit sotanghon*. Others are made from potato or sweet potato starch. Tapioca (cassava) shreds are another vegetable starch creation.

Nopales (Mexican) Leaves or pads of prickly pear cactus, these are somewhat similar to green beans but slightly tart in taste. They are steamed, diced, and added to scrambled eggs or tossed with tomato, onion, and vinaigrette. *Nopales* are available canned, bottled, pickled, and sometimes fresh. If you buy fresh you should look for firm, thin ones, and you need to clean them. Use tongs to hold them and a gloved hand to wield the knife on the little half-buried thorns. Just slice off the little bumps that contain them. Also discard the base.

Nopales have a slimy, okralike aspect that Mexican cooking tends not to appreciate. Commonly they are rinsed after boiling to get rid of the juice, or if stewed, the liquid is cooked down until it evaporates, taking the slime with it. The oval cactus fruits are also eaten. See also **Tunas.**

RECIPE REFERENCE: Nopales en Blanco, *The Art of Mexican Cooking,* p. 176.

Nori, laver (Japanese, Korean, European) The seaweed used in sushi wrapping, greenish black with a crumpled paper texture and mild flavor. Nori is also used in deep-fried dishes. When toasted over dry heat it becomes crisp and aromatic. Nori can be bought pretoasted in Japanese markets as *yaki nori* or powdered as *ao nori*. Known as *laver* in Europe, it is also a traditional vegetable of coastal Ireland and England, where it is reduced to a purée, mixed with oatmeal, and cooked on a griddle to make laver bread, a breakfast staple served with bacon and poached fish. It is best to freeze it for long-term storage.

Nuoc mam, nam pla, patis, petis (Vietnamese, Thai) Light brown, clear, and delicate in flavor, produced from saltwater fish, primarily anchovies, and used both in cooking and as a table seasoning. A primary ingredient of the Vietnamese dipping sauces for spring rolls and dressings for many salads, it undergoes a remarkable alchemy on the palate, giving a light, almost refreshing savor in contrast to its funky smell. Brands abound in any Asian grocery. You don't generally find small bottles, but it's pretty cheap and it keeps basically forever. I like the brand Fat Boy, as much for the label as for superior taste. We once named a pickup truck in its honor. See also, **Fish sauce.**

~ O ~

Okara (Japanese) The high-protein, rather tough residue left behind during tofu making. It is used in soups, vegetable dishes, and salads. You may be able to find it at Asian markets that make or market fresh tofu.

Okra, bamia, gumbo (Indian, Caribbean, African) An American Southerner might guffaw at the idea of including a basic like okra in a book of unfamiliar ingredients, but it's plenty exotic where I live. Slippery and glutinous once cut and cooked, it is one of the foods many love to hate. It is originally African, where its slithery attributes are much prized. The vegetable itself is a dull green, shaped rather like a jalapeño, but with ridges and a pointier end. Besides being big in the American South, stewed, fried, or as an ingredient in gumbo, it is very popular in the Caribbean. Breadfruit (or cornmeal) and okra make *coo-coo*. Plantain and okra make *fufu*. The name *bamia* refers to a popular Egyptian meat and vegetable stew, as well as to okra itself. If you are curious about okra but nervous about its texture, head for an Indian cookbook, where the pods are commonly either used whole or sliced and crisp-fried, treatments that do not bring out their slippery qualities. Indian cooking makes good use of okra in mixed curries or on its own in dishes such as the popular *dahi kadhi*, in which small whole okras are simmered in a mixture of spiced yogurt and chickpea flour.

RECIPE REFERENCE: **Dahi Kadhi,** *The Great Curries of India,* p. 146.

Olives (European, North African, Middle Eastern, Latin American)
Native to the eastern Mediterranean, olives have been cultivated for some 5,000 years, and some orchards are over 1,000
years old. The olive fruit contains a bitter glycoside which has
to be removed or converted before it is palatable. The most
common commercial curing method is to soak the olives a few
days in a lye solution and then put them in a brine solution for
flavor, resulting in the standard green Spanish olive or the mild,
dead-ripe black California olive (which tastes about as much
like an olive as a maraschino does like a cherry). The more flavorful cures of imported specialty olives result from one or a
combination of the other curing methods—in oil, water, salt,
and brine. The interplay of olive variety and type and length of
cure results in the hundreds of regional olive specialties, from
tangy green *naflions* to dry-cured, rich black Moroccan olives,
packed in brine with hot peppers.

Olive terminology is confusing, since it may refer to overlap-
ping categories of olive variety, region, and method of cure. It is
possible and necessary to distinguish basic types, in order to
match the flavor to the cuisine. Beyond that, searching out the
fine points by trial and error is going to be more rewarding than
any amount of reading.

Kalamata Dark purple and almond shaped with pungent flavor
and almost crunchy texture, grown in the Southwestern Pelo-
ponnese. *Kalamatas* are slit, brine cured, and then packed in

vinegar. *Kalamatas* are popular in Arabic cuisine, and are sometimes sold in a brine with Moroccan preserved lemons.

Atalanti, Royal A round Greek olive of variable size and color, from light brown to dark brown to red. They are slit, salt-brine cured and then kept in a vinegar and oil mixture, and are similar in flavor to the *kalamata*.

Amfissa Round and black, with a nutty sweet taste, from the central mainland of Greece.

Green Large and crunchy with mild flavor, from various Ionian islands.

Cracked green Made by cracking unripe green olives, placing them in water for several weeks to leach out the glycosides, and then storing them in brine. Some versions are very bitter. Middle Eastern groceries sell them in brine with hot green peppers.

Black, Thassos Small, wrinkled, dry-cured olives with a strong flavor, from Thassos in Greece.

Naflion A dark green, cracked olive which is cured in salt brine and then packed in olive oil. It is crisp in texture and zippy in flavor, without the richness of a ripe olive.

Nyon A small, wrinkly, green/black olive from the Nyon region of France. It is dry-salt cured and rubbed with oil, with an intense, rather bitter flavor that goes well with the sweet cooked onions in *pissaladiere*. It is also a source of quality French olive oil.

Niçoise Small roundish dark olives, with large pits. Salt brine cured and wonderful, they are the essential flavor in *salade Niçoise*.

Picholine A named French variety, usually picked green and salt brine cured with a mild flavor.

Moroccan Round, large (though not colossal), and black. These are salt brine cured and packed with herbs.

Moroccan dry-cured A ripe, dry-salt cured olive, and therefore black, wrinkled, and intense in flavor.

Middle Eastern green Often sold in brine with hot peppers or mixed with olive oil. Small, tender, and wonderful, this olive may be packed with herbs.

Ponentine A small, narrow, purple-black olive from Italy, salt-brine cured and packed in vinegar.

Sicilian-style Californian Firm green olives, packed in vinegar brine with hot peppers.

Orange blossom water, mazahar (North African, Middle Eastern, Indian, European) Diluted extract of the blossoms of the bitter orange tree, which line the streets of Marrakech and are common elsewhere in North Africa and in Spain. Used in fruit and vegetable salads (beet and cumin; orange, date and cinnamon; radish and orange; and Moroccan carrot salad) in North Africa and across the Mediterranean in Provence. It is also a common addition to couscous and to the almond and pastry dessert, gazelle's horns. The smell is intoxicatingly sweet and evocative. I'm always tempted to put a little in the salad and a little more behind my ears.

RECIPE: North African Beet Salad

> 3 medium beets (about 1 pound), boiled, peeled, and
>   sliced in julienne strips
> 2 tablespoons sugar
> 4 tablespoons lemon juice
> $^1/_2$ teaspoon ground cumin (preferably freshly ground
>   from whole seeds)
> 4 tablespoons olive oil
> 2 teaspoons orange blossom water

Mix all ingredients together and chill for an hour. Serves 6.

Ortanique (Caribbean) A modern cross between a sweet orange
and a tangerine, hence *or*(ange)-*tan*(gerine)-(un)*ique*. Juicy and
orange-sized, with tangerinelike skin and a flavor that combines
the two. It is grown commercially in the Caribbean.

Oyster sauce (Chinese) A sweetened sauce made from fermented
oysters, hoisin and soy sauces, and sherry. I can't taste the oysters but maybe I bought the wrong brand. Oyster sauce is popular in Cantonese cooking.

◈ P ◈

Palaver sauce, palava sauce (African) A West African favorite with
many variations—made with greens, chiles, palm oil, fish, *egusi*,
and often beef, tripe, pigs feet, and/or chicken. As you might
guess, the combination is spicy, oily, and strongly flavored.

Serve it with *fufu* or, less traditionally, over rice. It is sold canned in some specialty markets; it's expensive, but also distinctive and delicious, and a little goes a long way.

Palm butter, cream of palm fruits (African) Creamy, pale yellow, and highly saturated liquid from pounding and boiling palm nuts. It's sold in African markets to be used with fish, meat, and seafood. It is immortalized in a Liberian folk song, "Chicken is Nice (with Palm Butter and Rice)," that used to get play on the coffee house circuit.

Palm nut oil, dende oil (African, Latin American) A solid shortening made from palm oil. Both the color and the flavor, somewhat reminiscent of strong olive oil, are a signature of West African cooking, where it is used to add color and flavor to vegetable and rice dishes, and added often in astonishing quantities to stews. It traveled with the African diaspora to Brazil, where it is used inventively in combination with the indigenous seafood, tomatoes, and peppers popular in Bahian cooking.

———————————⋅≈ঃ———————————

RECIPE: Bahian Fish with Palm Oil
Modified from Moqueca de Peixe, *The Book of Latin American Cooking,* pp. 87–88

> 2 pound fillet of red snapper or other firm, mild fish
> 2 medium onions, chopped
> 1 chile de arbol or other small hot pepper, seeded and chopped
> 2 medium tomatoes, chopped
> 2 cloves garlic, chopped
> 3 tablespoons chopped cilantro
> $^1/_2$ cup coconut milk
> salt
> 4 tablespoons lemon or lime juice
> 3 tablespoons palm oil

Cut fish into 2-inch pieces and place in a large bowl. Combine onions, peppers, tomatoes, garlic, cilantro, salt, and lemon or lime juice, in a blender or food processor and blend briefly. Pour the mixture over the fish and marinate for at least one hour. Transfer fish and marinade to a saucepan, add coconut milk, and simmer until fish is done, 8 to 10 minutes. Add palm oil and heat through. Serve with rice. Serves 6.

Palm sugar, jaggery, gula mérah (Indian, Pan-Asian) Coarse brown sugar refined from the sap of the *kitul* palm or the coconut palm. It is sold in Southeast Asian and Indian markets, either as a paste or in blocks for grating. It looks and tastes like a mild maple sugar and is used in main dishes as well as in desserts and melted in tea. A reasonable substitute is Latin American *panela,* which is made from sugar cane and lacks some of the distinctive taste but does have the right texture. Supermarket brown sugar is acceptable but not the same. Some sugar sold as jaggery is actually coarse brown cane sugar. Once you've tasted them side by side you'll be able to tell the difference. See also **Panela.**

RECIPE REFERENCE: **Fish with Ginger Sauce,** *Fire & Spice,* p. 87.

Palm vinegar (Philippine) A mild, greenish vinegar made from palm sap and used in adobo sauces. It is a little stronger than Japanese rice vinegar, but not as strong as cider vinegar. Rice vinegar is a good substitute.

Pancit (Philippine) *Pancit* is the generic term for "noodles." *Pancit canton* is a round Chinese-style soft wheat noodle, which is precooked and dried for use in soups and stir fries. *Pancit mami* is a flat Chinese-style egg noodle. *Pancit miki* is similar but is made with less egg. *Pancit miswa* is a fine wheat noodle that cooks in seconds.

Pandanus, rampa, screwpine, daun pandan, kewra, vanilla leaf (Indian, Indonesian, Southeast Asian, Sri Lankan) A member of the lemongrass family, this aromatic, spear-shaped leaf is used rather like vanilla, to add a flowery flavor (and a green color) to sweets, ice cream, baked goods, and rice. The leaves themselves are not eaten but are removed before serving (or sometimes they are pounded, mixed with water, and put through a strainer), and the resulting green liquid is stirred into doughs or used to color *cendol,* a Balinese coconut milk drink popular with tourists. Pandanus is sold in most Asian markets, sometimes fresh but also frozen, canned, or in a tube in a concentrated paste. The flowers, which have a strong, sweet aroma, are distilled into a cooking essence. See also **Ruh kewra.**

Pan dulce (Mexican) Big puffy bread pastries with an array of glazes and coatings. These are sold at the counter in many Mexican groceries and are ideal for dipping into a breakfast *café con leche.*

Panela, rapadura (Latin American) An unrefined dark-brown cane sugar that is sold in cakes or cones. It has a caramel flavor, less sweet and more intense than supermarket brown sugar. It is eaten plain as little candies, or used in desserts either as sugar or the base for syrups. The rich flavor blends well with the blandness of cassavas, plantains, and other starchy bases for many Latin desserts.

Panir (Indian) A fresh white cheese curd much used in cooking, as it retains its shape when heated. It serves the same role as tofu, a mild-tasting, high-protein foil for savory sauces and condiments. Sometimes it is crumbled and baked with rice, boosting the protein content without greatly altering the taste. Available both fresh and frozen in cubes in most Indian groceries, it is also easy to make at home. Some recipes suggest substituting ricotta for *panir,* but the two are not really comparable in texture. Mexican *queso fresco* might be a better choice. See also **Queso Fresco.**

Panko (Japanese) Prepackaged bread crumbs to use in deep frying. There is nothing magically Japanese about them, but they do have a coarser texture than most American bread crumbs, and they are convenient.

Papadum (Indian) Thin round "chips" of lentil and/or rice flour, sometimes flavored with chiles, garlic, or spices. They look like very skinny tortillas and are sold in packs in Indian stores. Toast them on a dry skillet, gas flame, or stovetop. They are just a bit leathery when first toasted, but they will crisp up as they cool. The uncooked ones will keep indefinitely without refrigeration. These are great with rice and maybe a *raita* for a simple lunch, or crumbled as a garnish over rice. They also can be deep fried for just a few seconds, which makes them puff up and change color, but they are plenty good just toasted.

Papaya, fruta bomba, pawpaw (Latin American, Caribbean, Southeast Asian, Indonesian) Columbus called papaya the "fruit of angels," and Spanish and Portuguese sailors brought starts from the Caribbean to other tropical climes. In the field, it looks like an enormous brussels sprout, with the fruits clustered some twenty feet high along the top of the unbranched trunk. Sometimes the large, intricately cut leaves are boiled as a vegetable (they are reputed to taste like dandelion greens) or used as a wrapping for marinating meat, to impart both flavor and tenderness. A first truly ripe papaya is a life-altering experience for many northerners, but in their native lands papayas may be taken for granted, so much so that cooks often purposely pick them unripe to use as a vegetable. This use was a big shock to me at first report, reminding me of the appalled reaction when I mentioned to an acquaintance in Cuba that we have so many apples in Washington State that we use the windfall to fatten cattle. (While traveling in Cuba we also learned to stick with the local usage, *fruta bomba,* because the word *papaya* has been appropriated by Cubans as slang for the female genitalia.)

The crunchy, unripe papayas are used as a vegetable in Southeast Asian salads. Asian markets sell them frozen, imported from Thailand, and sometimes fresh from Hawaii or Mexico. They have a mild, slightly astringent taste and are pale green inside. Seeds of unripe papaya should be white. If they are black, the fruit is too mature for these uses. Green papaya is also the traditional tenderizer used to prepare tandoori chicken, giving it a bit of flavoring in addition to its famous texture.

Pasilla chile, chile negro, chile pasa (Latin American) A dried chile that looks like a large, dark prune. Favored in Guatemalan and Mexican cooking. When fresh, it has green/black skin and is called *chile chilaca.* The flavor is pleasant and moderately hot. Some markets give this name to green *chile poblanos,* which are in fact much milder. *Anchos* or *mulattos* make better substitutions.

Pekmez, grape syrup, grape molasses (Turkish) Grape juice boiled down to a thick syrup; it plays somewhat the same role as pomegranate molasses in Eastern Mediterranean cooking.

Pepitas (Mexican, Guatemalan) Pumpkin seeds, used in Mexico and Guatemala since pre-Columbian times. The small ones are called *chincillas.* They are grown extensively in the Yucatán, where Mayan cooking techniques still hold sway. Toasted and ground, hulled or whole, they are used in many moles, *pepiánes,* and *pozoles.* Sometimes they are cooked hulls and all, as in *pepian de Oaxaca,* a chicken soup. Mixed with syrup, they make a hard candy called *palanqueta*, which is similar to peanut brittle. Ground and cooked, they are used to make *quesitos de zanahoria*. These "little carrot cheeses" are intriguing on several counts. Anyone who has encountered Central American street food will recognize the genre of intensely sweet, somewhat mealy candies, often Day-Glo colored (although not in this recipe). Another interest is the cultural kinship between this and many Middle Eastern and Indian *halvahs* and *barfis*, which also use nuts or seeds reduced to a soft fudge through long simmering. There is even *halvah* that is also based on carrots. It seems clear that the Middle Eastern almond pastes and *halvahs*, which moved to Spain with the Moors and hence to the New World with the conquistadors, have been translated here from almond to squash seed. See also **Mazapan.**

———————— *3*————————

RECIPE: **Quesitos de Zanahoria**
False Tongues and Sunday Bread, p. 329.

> 3/4 cup squash seeds
> 2 cups water
> 1 pound (4 cups) grated carrots
> 2 1/2 cups milk
> 4 egg yolks
> one 4-inch stick cinnamon
> 2 cups sugar
> 1/4 teaspoon almond extract
> ground cinnamon
> 1 tablespoon milk, if needed

Soak seeds in water for an hour and drain. Process carrots, seeds, and milk together in a blender until smooth. Add egg yolks during blending. Heat mixture in a large saucepan with cinnamon stick and sugar. Simmer over low heat, stirring frequently, for about an hour or until paste comes away from sides and bottom of pan. Remove cinnamon.

Remove pan from heat and beat the mixture with a wooden spoon for 2 minutes. The cooled paste should pulverize when rubbed between the fingers. Knead half the mixture with a few drops of milk, as though it were bread dough. Add a few drops of almond extract. Knead the other half in the same way.

Make round cakes $1^1/2$ inches in diameter and $1/4$ inch thick. Dip both sides in cinnamon and rub it around the edges. Wrap each one in wax paper. They taste better the next day. Makes about 30 little cakes.

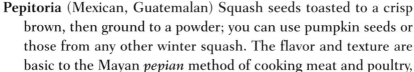

Pepitoria (Mexican, Guatemalan) Squash seeds toasted to a crisp brown, then ground to a powder; you can use pumpkin seeds or those from any other winter squash. The flavor and texture are basic to the Mayan *pepian* method of cooking meat and poultry, in which the meat is first boiled in plain water and then cooked in a sauce thickened with ground seeds. It's also excellent just sprinkled on dishes such as sautéed oysters.

Pepper leaves, la-lot (Thai, Vietnamese) A roundish, crinkly leaf from a cousin of the plant that produces black peppercorns. Sometimes sold fresh on the stem in Southeast Asian markets, they are used as wrappers for marinated meat and seafood and also in soups and vegetable stir fries. Perilla leaves are a good substitute or, in a pinch, well-rinsed grape leaves. See also **Perilla.**

RECIPE REFERENCE: **Beef Grilled in La-Lot Leaves (Bo Gai La-Lot)**, *The Simple Art of Vietnamese Cooking,* p. 158.

Pepperoncini, Tuscan peppers (Italian) Small, pointed chiles, generally red but sometimes green, with a mildly hot, slightly sweet flavor. They are most often sold pickled, in supermarkets as well as specialty stores.

Pequin chile, birdseye, bird chile (Latin American, Asian) Very small, very hot chile of the tabasco type, popular in Oaxaca, Mexico, where it usually is sold pickled or dried and ground, and in Southeast Asia, where it is used fresh (both green and red), dried, and in bottles with garlic and vinegar in the ubiquitous regional hot sauces. These really are too small to remove seeds and membranes effectively, so they are going to be hot no matter what. If they are too much for your palate, you could substitute a jalapeño or other somewhat milder chile. Otherwise, cayennes or tepíns are comparable.

Perilla, shiso (green), beefsteak plant (red), (Japanese) Aromatic leaves from the mint family, sold fresh in bunches in Asian markets, and pickled with or without ginger. Gardeners can order the seeds and grow their own. The two colors have different uses. Green is used as a tempura garnish and chopped leaves are added to salads, sashimi, and sushi. Red is less fragrant and is used to make *umeboshi* and other pickles; and the pickled leaves are used to wrap and flavor other foods. *Aoshisonomi* *zuke,* a mixture of chopped *shiso,* cucumber, and melon, pickled in citric acid, is sold in plastic packets in Japanese markets, ready to use as a garnish and to add to some of the heavier noodle dishes. I like to cook a flavored *somen* in chicken stock with a little miso and chopped ginger, and then sprinkle with *aoshisonomi zuke* and *sansho.*

Persimmon (Japanese) One of the most beautiful of fruits, persimmons are displayed on ancient Japanese crests as well as at table. Different varieties vary in shape and texture, but all are a clear orange inside and out. *Hachiyas* are teardrop shaped, with soft flesh. *Fuyus* are smaller, shaped like flat little pumpkins, and stay firm when ripe. The flavor when ripe is rich, smooth, and wonderful. When underripe it's a different, highly astringent story. Persimmons will continue to ripen off the tree for a few days, but they don't keep well. Asian markets sell them fresh and sometimes dried. In the United States, they are often used in sweetbreads and puddings. In Asia they generally are eaten out of hand.

Phed mak (Thai) A very hot, yellow chile sauce, sold bottled in Asian groceries. Not for the novice chile eater, who might rather start with the mildest grade of Thai *sriracha* sauce. See also **Sriracha.**

Pickled eggplant (Middle Eastern) If you're lucky, you live within shopping distance of a deli that has a bucket full of these very small, highly spiced eggplants, floating in a sour brine with chunks of red pepper. Serve with mild white cheese and good bread and you will be happy.

Pickled ginger, amazu shoga, hajikama su-zuje, beni shoga (Japanese) *Amazu shoga* is pink, sold sliced in vacuum packs or bottled in larger pieces and used as a sushi garnish and with grilled fish or chicken. It keeps indefinitely when refrigerated. The pinkness is a natural reaction to the sweet-and-sour brine. *Hajikama su-zuke* is similar in taste and usage, but is made of young ginger roots, pickled whole. It is a paler pink (the name means "blushing.") *Beni shoga* is red pickled ginger. Used with seasoned rice dishes.

Pigeon peas (African, Latin American, Indian) These flavorful, rather mealy peas may win the prize for the most common names, among them *toor dal, toovar dal, arhar dal, split yellow peas, red gram, gandules, gunga peas, guga,* and *goongoo.* Originally from Africa (or possibly India; botanists are debating), they are now widespread along the paths of the African diaspora, being especially popular in the Caribbean, where they are valued both as food and for the nitrogen-fixing properties of the perennial shrub that bears them. Rice and pigeon peas is a popular Caribbean dish, as is a ground pigeon-pea dumpling. They are puréed with coconut milk to make Nigerian *frejon* and Kenyan *mbaazi,* and elsewhere in West Africa ground and seasoned with onion and cayenne and made into fritters called *akara.* Often available dried and sometimes fresh (which are quicker to cook but a pain to shell), they are also sold canned in Latin American markets. Like many legumes, they do not freeze well, so canned beans are a better choice. Black-eyed peas are a reasonable substitute. Pigeon peas are not the same as the yellow split peas they somewhat resemble, and will not cook up the same way.

Pine nuts, pignoli, fistik, piñones (Mediterranean, Mexican, Chinese, Japanese, Korean) There are two main varieties of this pricy treat, probably best known as an ingredient in pesto. The Mediterranean ones are a little smaller and milder. The Chinese ones generally cost a bit less and have a slightly resinous aftertaste that is not to everyone's taste. The difference is not extreme, however. Try a taste test to see if it matters to you. In Turkey, pine nuts are used extensively in fillings for dolmas, fish, and *borek* as well as in pilaf. In Korea they are used to make gruel, ground up in sweet cakes, and used as a garnish.

Pine seed oil (European) A specialty salad oil made of pine nuts, also used as a dipping sauce for artichokes. If you grow your own artichokes, maybe you can afford to buy this oil to dip them in.

Pinol (Central American) Dry corn kernels, which are toasted before grinding to a powder and used to thicken sauces for chicken or turkey. This is one of the indigenous food techniques of Central America, from long before the arrival of Cortés.

Piripiri (African) A long, red, very hot chili, and also the name of the national dish of Mozambique, which uses them as part of a marinade for grilled chicken, meat, or fish. The name means "penis" in Swahili, inspired by its shape and potency. This meaning came to North America with African slaves and survives in some parts of the rural American South, so watch your language as you shop. A seasoned oil and a ground spice of the same name may sometimes be found in African markets but are not used in the Mozambiquan dish, which actually uses a versatile marinade mixture called *shatta*. See also **Shatta.**

Plantains (Pan-Asian, Caribbean, Latin American) Big, not so sweet, cooking bananas, often used as a vegetable. Plantains are one of the most prolific of all carbohydrate-producing crops—an area of ground that can produce 50 pounds of wheat or 100 of potatoes could carry as much as 4,000 pounds of plantains. Often they are simply boiled, jazzed up with spices, onions and pepper, and served with meat; or they may be sliced thin and deep-fried like potato chips. Chopped beef and plantains are the main ingredients of the famous Puerto Rican dish *piononos*. It is important to match your plantain to the recipe. Green ones are hard enough to slice thin and deep fry. They also can be boiled like potatoes or thoroughly cooked in a casserole. But if you try (as I did in my innocence) cooking them in a syrup to absorb flavor, they get tough and rubbery without acquiring much taste—better for patching radiators than for good eating. Ripe plantains are the ones for sweet dishes and short sautéing. Plantains aren't eaten raw in the tropics where sweeter bananas abound, but the truth is that a ripe one, at least of the smaller varieties, is just as tasty raw as the mealy, green-picked bananas usually sold in North America.

Poblano chile (Latin American, Middle Eastern, Mediterranean) A wonderful big chile with just a bit of heat. Used for Mexican *chiles rellenos* and also popular in Arab states, where a similar dish, *fifil mahshi bil kuzbara,* uses a similar combination of mild white cheese, cilantro, and tomato sauce, but is baked rather than fried in a batter coating. *Poblanos* are particularly popular in Turkey, where they are roasted and peeled, then used with grilled meats. (The chiles sold as *pasillas* in some California markets are also *poblanos*.)

Pomegranate, nar, nar suyu, anardana grenadine (European, Indian, Middle Eastern) The fruit, with its rosy casing, intricate chambers and jewel-like seeds, is a feature of love stories and poetry throughout the Arab world. It is one of the fruits of paradise referred to in the Koran as a proof of God's abundance, and indeed Middle Eastern and Eastern European cooks make much more use of pomegranate than is common in North America, although pomegranate trees grow and bear fruit up into northern California. The fresh juice is used in Turkish and North African cooking and in other regions where Arab culture has traveled. (Laurens van der Post writes of a dinner in Zanzibar, where a hot roasted chicken was finished by simmering it in a mixture of pomegranate juice and water, and then thickened with ground walnuts to serve as gravy; a very similar Iranian dish is called *fesenjon*.) The Turkish sauce, *muhmmara*, uses the same pomegranate/walnut combination. The famous Persian soup *ash* also gets part of its sweet-and-sour flavor from the juice. Pomegranate seeds are used fresh in dips such as Yemeni *akeel*. The dried seeds, both whole and powdered, are sold in Indian markets as a souring agent for curries. A sour variety of pomegranate is popular in Turkey and Eastern Europe, and recipes from those areas calling for fresh juice may need the addition of lemon if made with the sweeter North American fruit. See also **Dibs rumman.**

RECIPE REFERENCE: **Ash,** *Flatbreads and Flavors,* p. 60.

Porcini mushrooms, cep, cepes (European) Large wild mushrooms of the genus *Boletes* with distinctive spongy gills. Fresh ones don't keep well; they generally are sold dried, which also serves to concentrate their wonderful flavor. Available in many supermarkets and European delis, boletes are common in many North American woodlands, but you should not collect your own without a good mushroom guidebook or an experienced partner, as some species of this prolific genus are poisonous.

Potato flour, potato starch, bot khoai tay (European, Vietnamese) A very fine powder, used as a binder for meat mixtures such as Vietnamese pâtés. Cornstarch can be substituted. It's available in supermarkets as well as in Asian groceries.

Potato leaves (African) Don't improvise with your garden potato leaves, which are poisonous. These are sweet potato leaves, available canned in some African markets and used in soups and stews.

Preserved cabbage, Tientsin preserved vegetables, cu cai hu, chou conserve (Chinese, Vietnamese, Thai) Salt-pickled Chinese cabbage, sold in distinctive red glazed pots from China as well as in plastic tubs. Use it as is, in small portions, as a snack, garnish, or soup addition. It keeps pretty much forever as long as you keep it cool and covered.

Prick dong (Thai) No jokes now. This is a bottled chile sauce combining heat, sweet, and salt, and made from chiles, onions, apricots, lemon, garlic, and vinegar, in various versions. Basically we're talking about a highly evolved ketchup here.

Pumpkin seed oil (Central European) Pumpkin or other winter squash seeds are toasted and then pressed. The resulting oil has a pleasant nutty flavor that goes well sprinkled over steamed or boiled vegetables. It is used primarily in Austria.

❧ Q ❧

Quail eggs (Chinese, Southeast Asian) For me these fall into the "too pretty to eat" category. Tiny, cream colored, with random markings reminiscent of ink brush paintings. They are sold fresh in some Asian markets and are more generally available canned. They are used boiled, whole or halved, and the raw yolks sometimes appear as a garnish for sushi. Fresh ones are preferable, as you would expect.

Queso fresco (Latin American) A mild white Mexican cheese with a high melting point, *queso fresco* can be cubed and added to tacos and enchiladas or grated on top of tostadas and other dishes. It serves some of the same purpose as tofu in Asian cooking, soaking up stronger flavors from the surrounding dish and providing a contrast to crisper textures. It's available in Latin American markets and in most supermarkets where there is a Mexican-American community. The Indian cooking cheese *panir* is similar. See also **Panir.**

Quince (European, Middle Eastern) Seldom available fresh, quince is too puckery to eat raw but combines wonderfully with other flavors when cooked, as in the recipe for lamb and fresh quince ragout given here. The hard, green-skinned fruits are popular in Turkish and other Eastern Mediterranean dishes, where they are mixed with meat or served in a cooked compote with other fruits, including apple and pomegranate. As the sweet paste *ate*, quince has made its way from the Arabic countries to Spain to Latin America. A traditional Romanian combination is boiled meat with stewed quinces and onion; the addition of sugar gives it the sweet-and-sour taste popular in much Eastern European cooking. The standard ornamental flowering quince tree can produce perfectly good quince fruit, although mine does not fruit reliably. See also **Ate.**

———————————❦———————————

RECIPE: **Lamb and Fresh Quince Ragout**
The Great Book of Couscous, p. 12.

>   3 pounds quince
>   salt to taste
> $1/4$ cup vegetable oil
>   2 pounds lamb stew meat
>   1 medium onion, chopped ($1/2$ cup)
>   5 sprigs parsley, chopped
> $1/2$ teaspoon black pepper
>   1 teaspoon sweet paprika
> $1/2$ teaspoon turmeric
>   1 cup tomato, chopped
>   2 cups water
>   2 teaspoons ground cinnamon
> $1/4$ cup sugar

Quarter quinces, remove seeds, cores, and stems, and then cube. Cover with water, add $1/4$ teaspoon salt, and cook 20 minutes until tender/soft. Drain and save. Put oil, lamb, onion, parsley, salt, pepper, paprika, and turmeric in a big skillet and stir-fry over low heat for 5 minutes.

Add tomato and water and cook 30 minutes or more, until meat is soft. Add quinces, cinnamon, and sugar. Shake pan to mix and simmer everything together over low heat for 10 minutes until sauce is thick. Arrange lamb and sauce on a platter and place quinces in a mound on top. Serves 6–8.

———————— ᦾ ————————

Quinoa (South American) A domesticated relative of lambs'-quarters, drought tolerant and hardy and nutritious, all of which helps to make up for its labor-intensive harvest and preparation. Quinoa seeds are small and round and have a natural coating of saponin, a soapy compound that tastes lousy and isn't good for you. Most commercially purchased products have had the saponin removed so you can proceed straight to cooking, but check the instructions carefully. Quinoa seeds are good pan-roasted and then cooked like millet. They have a rich nutty taste and do well as a breakfast porridge or as an alternative to rice. Some natural foods stores sell quinoa pasta. Try cooked quinoa as a substitute for bulgur in tabouli.

ᦾ R ᦿ

Ramen, ba mee, hokkien mee, Chinese egg noodles (Japanese, Chinese, Southeast Asian) Egg noodles made from soft wheat, used mostly in hot soups. Sold dried, fresh, or prefried and dried, as in the ubiquitous ramen soup mixes that crowd grocery shelves in both supermarkets and Asian groceries. Low-fat ramen mixes, in which the noodles have not been fried, are increasingly available. Fresh is still better. Ramen soup is a traditional street food in Japan, particularly on the chilly northern island of Hokkaido.

Ras el hanoot (North African) I have seen several translations of the Arabic names of this spice mixture, all of which imply the range of possible flavors involved. *Ras el hanoot* is the Moroccan equivalent of masalas in Indian cooking, a ground spice mixture with a hundred variations. A measure of the sophistication of North African cooking, these carefully chosen mixtures accentuate and complement the sweetness and the heat in *tagines* and couscous as well as transforming fruit salads and compotes from ordinary to tantalizing. A highly abbreviated version is sold in Arabic markets as *quatre épices* and contains cumin, cinnamon, ginger, and nutmeg, with cumin predominating. Other mixtures may contain as many as fifty ingredients, including sweet spices, hot chiles, black pepper, ground rosebuds and orrisroot, turmeric, thyme, bay leaves, and lavender.

Recado (Mexican) A Yucatecan seasoning paste (or crumbly brick) combining *achiote,* oregano, salt, some sort of tart liquid (preferably Seville orange juice) and a variety of other ingredients. It's used to rub on meat, especially poultry, before cooking or to give color and flavor to braising liquid. Latin American markets sell *recados* of varying degrees of quality. Sometimes the *achiote* is too old, giving a harsh, dusty taste, and sometimes the paste has been extended with masa, which will quickly sour if not used right away. (Freeze any unused portion if masa is an ingredient.) If you buy one prepared, dilute with enough mild vinegar or bitter orange juice to make a paste. See also **Achiote condimentado.**

———————— ≈ƒ ————————

RECIPE: **Basic Recado**

    1 tablespoon dried oregano
    $1/2$ cup dried *ancho* or *poblano* chiles
    2 tablespoons annatto seeds
    4 teaspoons salt
    2 garlic cloves, chopped fine
    $1/4$ cup bitter orange juice or mild vinegar (palm vinegar
        would be good)
    1 cup fresh orange juice

Roast oregano in a dry skillet over medium heat until it is fragrant and beginning to turn brown. Transfer to a small bowl, let cool, and add chiles, achiote, and salt. Put these ingredients into a spice grinder or blender and process until finely ground. Mix in garlic and combine with orange juice and vinegar (if used). Makes about 1 $1/2$ cups.

———————— ≈ƒ ————————

Red bean-curd cheese (Chinese) Small, brick-red squares of soybean paste, about one inch thick. The pungent taste comes from fermentation with salt, rice, and rice wine. The color comes from annatto seeds. Bean-curd cheese is sold canned and in jars and is used as a seasoning, often with congees, vegetable dishes, and braised meats. Transfer any unused portion from its can to a non-reactive container for storage in the refrigerator.

Rice Rice is the true staff of life, sustaining more people than any other food. Like the olives of the Mediterranean and the noodles of Asia, it has hundreds of regional varieties and nearly as many cooking techniques, all passionately debated. Only a fraction of these types are available outside their regions, but even a small-town supermarket is likely to have enough variety these days to convey the essential characteristics of the great rice-based cuisines. Besides cooked rice grains, the world runs on rice noodles, rice flour (some glutinous, some not), rice wine and vinegar, roasted rice powder, rice paper wrappers for steamed foods, puffed rice, and flattened rice. More recent technology has added "converted rice," which is not bad, and precooked "instant rice," which does not deserve the name.

Each rice dish involves an interplay between the grain's characteristics and the cooking method. Fragrant Indian basmati rice is soaked before cooking, and then cooked without stirring and left to stand undisturbed, so that each long fragile grain will stand separate from its neighbors. Plump Italian *arborio* varieties are sautéed in oil or butter and then cooked with frequent additions of simmering stock to make a creamy, starchy matrix carrying the flavors of a risotto. Japanese rice is steamed into a slightly sticky mass with a congealed, slightly toasted layer on the bottom. Each result is as different as a bagel is from a croissant, and each is perfect for the cuisine at hand. You should check the listings for specific kinds of rice, but the basics are these:

Long-Grain Varieties The most common types grown and sold in North America, these are meant to cook up into light and fluffy separate grains. They are appropriate for Indian, Chinese, and Latin American dishes, as well as the pilafs and dolmas of Mediterranean and Middle Eastern cooking. Some Indian cooks recommend Uncle Ben's converted rice if basmati is not available, because the process used contributes to the separation valued in Indian dishes, as well as driving nutrients from the hull into the body of the grain.

Short-Grain Varieties These are suitable for "sticky rice" dishes—Japanese sushi and *donburi,* many Indonesian dishes, and puddings and other desserts. (Cal Rose is one supermarket standby.) Korean rice also should be short- to medium-grain and sticky, the better to handle with the traditional round, pointy Korean chopsticks. Sticky rice is also known as glutinous rice, though it contains no gluten. It is used for sweets in countries that use regular rice for main dishes, but it is the preferred staple in parts of Southeast Asia, especially Laos, Cambodia, and Vietnam.

Arborio and other medium-grain varieties These Mediterranean varieties occupy a sort of middle ground between long- and short-grain rice.

Flaked rice Flattened and parboiled short-grain rice, often tinted green. Sold in Asian groceries, it is used in puddings and other sweets and also to stuff poultry.

Brown rice Any rice variety that has not been hulled. Both short- and long-grain brown rice are sold in natural foods stores, as is brown basmati. Although definitely more nutri-

tious and higher in fiber, brown rice is not favored by any traditional cuisines I know of, partly no doubt because of its
long cooking times. (Other colored rices—red, black, and
pink—take their color from natural colorations of the inner
grain rather than the hull.)

Red rice (Chinese, French) A glutinous variety grown in China,
where it is less favored than white sticky rice, and also in the
swampy Camargue region of France, where it is marketed as a
specialty grain. It is slow-cooking and should be soaked first.

Rice flour Flour is made of both sweet (glutinous) and regular rice,
and the difference is important to many recipes. Sweet rice
flour may be easier to come by. *Mochiko* is one name for sweet
rice flour, used for *mochi, dim sum,* and cookies. It is also used
in Middle Eastern cooking to thicken puddings. The little rectangular boxes in supermarkets, recommended for making
white sauce, are made of sweet rice, as is most of what is sold
at Japanese stores. Regular rice flour is sold in Indian groceries
for making *dosa* and *pappadum.* Cream of Rice cereal is the supermarket version, but supermarket rice flour is too gritty for
many recipes. If you don't get the results you want, you may
need to seek out rice powder in an Asian or Middle Eastern grocery. See also **Mochi.**

RECIPE REFERENCE: **Hwajon,** *Flavours of Korea,* p. 170.

Rice powder, roasted (Vietnamese) Long-grained rice, pan-
roasted until golden brown and then ground fine. Used sprin-

kled on Vietnamese salads and on plain rice, and as a binder in fillings.

Rock sugar (Chinese) Pretty crystals of sugar, sometimes colored, sold in Asian markets. Used to give a glaze or shine to red cooked Chinese dishes and to make syrups for sweet soups and candied fruit.

Rose petals (Indian, Middle Eastern) Petals from the intensely fragrant damask roses are sun dried and then powdered for use as a meat marinade and in spice mixtures such as *ras el hanoot.* Used in Moslem meat dishes such as white *korma.* Iranian cooks mix them with mint and cucumbers and serve in cold soup with yogurt. See also **Ras el hanoot.**

Rose water, ruh gulab, gulab jal, gül (Indian, Middle Eastern, Eastern European) A diluted form of attar of roses. In India it's used to flavor *kheer,* a rice dessert, and for the refreshing yogurt drink, *lassi,* as well as an auspicious sprinkling on guests at weddings. It's also traditional in Turkish delight, Moroccan couscous, and any number of Middle Eastern salads. As a legacy of the Ottoman occupation of Eastern Europe, many cooks there use it in baking. A heavier version of rose essence and sugar syrup is known as *gulab sharbat;* it is diluted with water for a popular beverage and also used to make rose-flavored ice cream. Whole rose petals in heavy syrup are also sold canned in Indian markets.

Ruh kewra, kewra water (Indian) Bottled essence of the flower of the screwpine tree, used extensively in Moghul cooking, especially with meat and poultry, and with some sweets. Rose water is a reasonable substitute. The leaves of the same tree make a

popular Southeast Asian coloring and flavoring for sweets. See
Pandanus.

✺ S ✺

Salam leaves, Indonesian bay leaves, duan salam (Indian, Indonesian, Southeast Asian) These slender, three-inch leaves,
Eugenia polyantha, are dried and used to flavor soups, curries,
and rice dishes and in the high-powered Indonesian condiment
sambal bajak. They have a gentle taste and spicy aroma that
stands out in mild dishes and helps to modulate hot ones. They
are not the same as curry leaves; a bay leaf is a better substitute
if you can't find them in Asian markets. Bay leaves are more
strongly flavored, so you should cut the amount about in half.
See also **Sambal bajak.**

Salt fish (worldwide) One of the oldest known trade items, salt
fish traveled with the Roman legions and even earlier with
traders from the Middle East, valued as a way to preserve
abundant protein in easily portable form. Its use was given a
big boost by the spread of Christianity, whose Friday fast days
and Lenten observance required a steady supply of fish. (The
popularity of frog legs in many Catholic countries is another
legacy of religious observance, since they were classified as
fish, as were beaver tails once Catholic missionaries reached
North America.)

Being the most abundant catch, cod was the most common
dried fish, making a place for itself on every inhabited continent
and climate zone. Norwegians gutted cod by the millions and

hung them to dry on wooden racks, providing the people of the Middle Ages with *stokkfish,* a cheap and almost indestructible food reserve. Turning that staying power into something savory as well as sustaining has long been a challenge for cooks. For many Norwegians the answer is lutefisk, in which dried but unsalted cod is soaked first in water for a week and then in a mixture of potash lye, the resulting simmered dish turning into a sort of translucent fish jelly. Other methods include that one recommended by a fourteenth-century Paris merchant: "to beat it with a wooden hammer for a full hour and then set it to soak in warm water for a full two hours or more, then cook it and scour it very well . . . then eat it with mustard or soaked in butter." Salt cod is still common to Lenten and "lean" Christmas Eve dinners in Catholic Europe. One Niçoise version, typically sensuous despite its message of self-denial, involves a mixture of dried cod, garlic, potato, milk, and olive oil—lots of olive oil—blended, cooked briefly, and served in a puff pastry shell or in stuffed vegetables. Salt fish and ackee (see recipe under **Ackee**), is another smooth and delicious combination.

An Asian market may sell a bewildering variety of dried fish, from tiny whole ones to big slabs of cod or tuna. Even though it might keep ten years, it's better if it doesn't. It's best to avoid the weatherbeaten pieces. Cooking with salt fish requires planning. It needs long soaking to soften the fish and leach out the salt, followed by careful cleaning to remove tiny bones. After that, though, the recipes generally are simple. See also **Katsuobushi** and **Maldive fish.**

Sambaar powder, sambaar podi (Indian) The most popular generic masala of South Indian cooking. It is hotter than *garam masala*, and is designed for the spicy vegetable and lentil dishes of vegetarian Indian cuisine. It is widely available at Indian markets. Look for a can or a bottle in preference to a cardboard box, as the spices lose their potency when exposed to air. Its main ingredients are fenugreek, red and black pepper, mustard, and ground dal.

Sambal (Pan-Asian, Indonesian) *Sambal* is a generic name for any pastelike condiment made with chile. The authentic versions tend to be made with the chile seeds included and are very hot. There are dozens of varieties in Indonesian, Malaysian, and Sri Lankan cooking. Some of the more common, such as *sambal ulek,* are easy to find in Asian groceries and well-stocked supermarkets, and most are simple to make. See specific names for details.

Sambal bajak (Indonesian) High-powered cooked chile sauce, mellowed with sugar and ground nuts or coconut milk, and served with the famous Indonesian fried rice *nasi goreng.* It's also a nice addition to chicken soups, and I like it as a garnish for baked potatoes. It's available bottled in Asian markets, or you can make your own. Recipes vary markedly in their ingredients; I particularly like the one given here.

———————— ❧ ————————

RECIPE: **Sambal Bajak**
Southeast Asian Cooking, p. 37.

> 8 macadamia nuts or candlenuts
> $^1/_4$ pound fresh hot red chiles (bird chiles or serranos)
> 1 medium onion, quartered and peeled
> 4 cloves garlic, peeled
> $^1/_2$ teaspoon shrimp paste
> 1 tablespoon palm or brown sugar
> 2 tablespoons vegetable oil
> 1 *salam* leaf or curry leaf (optional)
> $^1/_4$ cup water

Pound nuts to a paste in a mortar; mince chiles, onion, and garlic, and add to mortar with the shrimp paste and sugar. Pound to a coarse paste. Or put it all in a food processor and blend, with a little water if necessary.

In a small skillet or pan, heat oil over medium heat. Add chile paste and salam leaf and cook, stirring, until fragrant. Add water and continue cooking until water has evaporated and oil begins to separate. Serve warm or at room temperature or store in a tightly covered jar in a cool place. Makes about 1 cup.

Sambal kacang, peanut sambal (Indonesian) Widely available bottled, and used for satay and other grilled meats, and *gado gado.* This is the most familiar Indonesian flavor for many people. Regional variations abound, but all contain ground peanuts, hot chiles, sweet and sour flavors (generally from palm sugar and tamarind), and soy sauce. Thai peanut sauce, by comparison, tastes more of soy and less of peanuts.

Sambal kacang kedele (Indonesian) A relish using dried soybeans, chiles, onion, garlic, and lime juice or tamarind.

Sambal kecap (Indonesian) A popular sauce for grilled vegetables; soy sauce augmented with onion, garlic, lime, and chiles.

Sambal terasi (Javanese) A very hot relish made from bird chiles with cooked shrimp paste, garlic, onion, and lime juice.

Sambal ulek, sambal oelek (Indonesian) Red paste of ground bird chiles, salt, and a bit of oil and vinegar. Many of the commercial versions are bottled in the Netherlands.

Sansho, Sichuan pepper, fagara (Chinese, Japanese) The fragrant dried reddish-brown berry of a Chinese prickly ash tree, whose use predates both black pepper and chiles. It's only the outside covering of the ripe seed that is collected and dried, which helps to explain why it's so expensive. (Unripe *sansho* seeds are called *mizansho* and are boiled down, seed coat and all, in a soy sauce mixture.) *Sansho* is used in Chinese five-spice powder, along with star anise, cloves, fennel, and cassia, and in Japanese *shichimi* (seven spices). It also is sold as a condiment on its own by roasting with sea salt and grinding the combination. If you get it fresh, you need to dry-roast it and then grind it to powder. Store it tightly covered or else the distinctive, flowery aroma will dissipate into the air. Its heat is gentle, not fierce, making it a wonderful seasoning for a mild fish that could be overwhelmed by stronger flavors. It is used with bean threads, cucumber, and carrot threads for a traditional Sichuan salad and in *guo fa,* a breakfast skillet bread. See also **Five-spice powder, Ki no mé,** and **Shichimi.**

RECIPE REFERENCE: **Guo Fa,** *Flatbreads and Flavors,* p. 93.

Sea cucumber, bêche de mer, iriko, trepang (Chinese) This is a soft-bodied marine creature from the intertidal area, a sort of stationary jellyfish. Its texture, a sort of firm jelly, is a recurring favorite in Cantonese cooking; shark fins and cellophane noodles share some of its characteristics, including its minimal flavor. This is an ingredient for banquets and other impressive occasions rather than for family meals and I personally would just as soon skip it. However, sea cucumbers can be purchased dried, and in some cases presoaked and ready to use, in most Chinese markets.

Sea urchin (Japanese, European) The sea urchin's spiny outside hides a tender center and delicate roe that are popular in Japan and in Europe along the Mediterranean. Both body and roe are eaten, either fresh or lightly cooked. The roe is golden. It is sometimes sold fresh in good fish markets and also is available bottled.

Semolina, farina, sooji (European, North African, Middle Eastern, Indian) The hard, low-starch flour made from the same durum wheat that becomes Italian pasta and couscous. Semolina is yellowish in color. Under a microscope it looks rocky, with none of the soft starch granules that can be seen sticking out of softer wheats. Cream of Wheat is made from farina, with added salt and preservatives, and can be substituted in recipes with a slight loss in quality. Recipes go back thousands of years. Cato the Censor, when he was not busy exhorting his fellow Romans to destroy Carthage, was collecting recipes for a sweet porridge made of semolina or spelt, another wheat variety. Semolina flour makes a fine Sicilian bread, North African pastry wrappers such as *malsouka,* and the popular Indian home dessert *sooji halwa,* as well as the fried Berber bread *l' harsha,* which is often sold as a street snack.

───────────── ᣟ ─────────────

RECIPE: L'Harsha
The Great Book of Couscous.

> 4 tablespoons butter
> 1 cup olive oil
> 2 pounds fine semolina flour
> 1 teaspoon salt
> 4 eggs, beaten
> $^1/_2$ cup water

Warm butter and oil together. Add remaining ingredients and mix, stirring vigorously. Knead 10 minutes. Divide into 8 pieces. Oil a medium skillet. Take a ball of dough and press into a round flat disk, a little more than $^1/_2$-inch thick. Fry over low heat about 10 minutes on each side until light brown. Repeat with remaining dough. Makes 8 rounds.

───────────── ᣟ ─────────────

Sen mee, hsan kyasan (Thai, Burmese) Dried rice vermicelli. See **Rice noodles,** listed under **Noodles.**

Serrano chile, chile japones, santaka, hontaka (Latin American, Caribbean, Pan-Asian) As the range of common names indicates, this small, slender chile shows up in kitchens around the planet and can be used whenever a hot chile is called for in a recipe. It is sold both fresh and dried. Fresh ones tend to be multicolored when ripe. There is not much depth to the taste; serranos are just plain hot.

Sesame leaves, kkaetnip (Korean) Available canned in Korean groceries. Used raw with rice, or stuffed and batter fried, serving somewhat the same role as grape leaves in Mediterranean cooking.

Sesame seeds, goma susam (Middle Eastern, Indian, Japanese, Chinese) In Japanese recipes, white unhulled seeds are *shiro goma*; white hulled seeds are *muki goma*; black seeds are *kuro goma*; black seeds plus salt are the popular seasoning *goma shio*. Store in airtight containers and dry-roast just before eating. Use white unless specified otherwise. See also **Tahini.**

Shaoxing, far jiu (Chinese, Vietnamese, Philippine) an amber-colored wine made with glutinous rice and millet, which often is used in Cantonese sauces. It is better if aged; ten years is standard. If you are going to buy it, go for the good stuff and avoid brands labeled as cooking wine. If not, a medium sherry is an acceptable, though not equivalent, substitute.

Shark fin (Chinese) If you are going to experiment with this high-price, low-taste example of Chinese haute cuisine (the standard joke is that it takes "three days to prepare and three minutes to eat") you may as well go the distance and buy it frozen and already prepared. The texture is gelatinous, with the muted crunch of a shark's cartilaginous "bones," and the flavor is vanishingly mild.

Shatta, piripiri sauce (African, Middle Eastern) A condiment in the Sudan and Mozambique, sometimes found in African and Middle Eastern markets. It can be used like a Southeast Asian sambal as a pick-me-up for soups, stews, and bland grains. It is commonly made with the fiery piripiri chile, hence the alternate name. Tabasco sauce with a bit of garlic added would make a reasonable substitute. See also **Piripiri**.

RECIPE REFERENCE: **Shatta**, *The von Welanetz Guide to Ethnic Ingredients*, 1982 edition, p. 115.

Shichimi, seven-spice mixture, shichimi togarashi (Japanese) An enlivening spice mixture used on noodle dishes and in soups. It's sold in expensive little shaker jars in Japanese markets, but a little does go a long way. It always contains *sansho* and sesame seeds. The other ingredients vary: seaweed, chile, tangerine or orange peel, poppy seeds, rape seeds, flax seeds, mustard seeds.

Shiitake, black mushroom, pyogo (Japanese, Chinese, Southeast Asian) These used to be sold only dried in most of North America, but shiitake growing has become something of a cottage industry, at least in my part of the Northwest, and fresh ones are now in the supermarkets. I prefer fresh for vegetable dishes and dried for soups. The dried ones have a much stronger flavor, so don't substitute straight across. They are good-looking mushrooms with a broad, flat cap and gills that darken to near black when dried. When shopping for dried ones, look for those with cracked tops and creamy flesh. Soak in warm water before using. They are ready when they're soft. Save the strongly flavored soaking water for soups.

Shirataki (Japanese) Clear, mild-tasting noodles made from devil's tongue root, called "white waterfall." See also **Konnyaku.**

Shrimp (dried), camarón seca, camarón mole, ébi (Chinese, Japanese, Latin American, Pan-Asian) These little shellfish morsels are one of the great common denominators of ethnic cuisine, found in all sorts of combinations practically worldwide. Dried prawns are also used, though they are not as common. They may be ground into fritter batter, toasted and added somewhat like bacon bits to vegetable dishes, and soaked and used in soup; sometimes they also show up as the main ingredient, as in the recipe from Sri Lanka given here, which traditionally uses a tiny shrimp sold as *coon.* Look for pink, plump ones, intact if possible; keep them tightly sealed, and store them in the refrigerator. The powdered *camarón* sold in Latin American markets does not have as much taste. Do not substitute the fermented shrimp or shrimp pastes of Asian cuisine, as the flavor is very different. See **Kimpira Gobo.**

Shrimp paste, kapi, bagoong, terasi, blachan, pazun ngapi (Burmese, Southeast Asian, Philippine, Chinese, Japanese) Brownish, dry paste or bottled concentrate made from fermented shrimp. It is available in bricks (dried), "fresh" (in jars), with a layer of solidified oil on top, or in precooked slices. The flavor is more concentrated than fish sauce and much more pungent than dried shrimp. It is used in Thai and Indonesian curries and extensively in Burmese cooking.

Shrimp paste is always cooked, either grilled or baked. It smells bad and tastes worse when raw, but when mixed with spices and cooked it is delicious, though assertive. One food writer recommends burning a scented candle to counteract the smell as you cook it. Chinese shrimp paste is said to be stronger than Thai, so be forewarned. It's a good idea to start with less than the recipe calls for, to allow for your own taste and for variations in strength. For a rewarding cross-cultural experience, try adding $1/4$ teaspoon of shrimp paste to your vegetable soup stock. I have struggled to get the rich taste I want in a vegetarian minestrone, and that touch of shrimp paste is just what's needed, if your principles allow. See also **Sambal terasi.**

————————•◦§————————

RECIPE: Baked Shrimp Paste (Ngapi Phoke)
The Burmese Kitchen, p. 56.

> 2 tablespoons shrimp paste
> 1 tablespoon semihot chile, thinly sliced
> 2 tablespoons lime juice

Put shrimp paste in a dish and shape into a small round cake about 3 inches in diameter and $1/4$ inch thick. Push your finger into the cake to make 8 depressions. Bake at 400°F for about 5 minutes, so that a light crust forms on top.

Remove from the oven and mash the paste. Add the chile and lime juice and mix well. Serve at room temperature with any type of Burmese curried dishes as well as rice dishes.

———————— ◦ç ————————

Shungiku, edible chrysanthemum, garland chrysanthemum, tong ho, shimizu, ssuka (Japanese, Chinese, Korean) Sold fresh in bundles, preferably with roots attached, these dark-green, finely cut leaves have a strong taste and a spicy, resinous odor. They also are easy to grow, although the flowers are nowhere near as impressive as their garden-variety cousins. The leaves taste best in fall, when cool weather mellows their flavor. Discard stems and flower buds. They don't keep long, and the flavor is not to everyone's taste, so it is wise to buy just a little, at least at first.

RECIPE REFERENCE: **Oyster Pot with Bean Broth (Kaki Nabe),** *At Home with Japanese Cooking,* p. 113.

Sichuan, Sichuan jah choy, Sichuan vegetable (Chinese) Chinese cabbage, cut in chunks and pickled with lots of red pepper. Sold canned, bottled, and/or in ceramic crocks. Hot, spicy, and salty; it needs to be rinsed before cooking, but you should store it unrinsed.

Sichuan chile sauce, la jiou, chile paste with garlic (Chinese) Hot fermented pepper paste, readily available in Chinese groceries and most supermarkets. There are many different varieties and degrees of heat. Some contain soybeans and other additions. It's used more in stir fries and as an ingredient in other sauces than as a table condiment. See also **Kochujang.**

Smen (North African, Middle Eastern) A seasoned, preserved butter, used in the classic Moroccan dish, *trid.* Unlike *ghee* and *nit-*

ter kibbeh, two other long-storage butters, *smen* is slightly fermented. "One either likes it or does not," writes food historian Copeland Marks. It will keep for years without refrigeration. See also **Ghee** and **Nitter kibbeh.**

Soba (Japanese) Thin buckwheat noodles, tan in color and coarser in texture than wheat spaghetti. They are sold for a lot in macrobiotic sections of natural foods stores and for a lot less in Asian markets. There are many varieties, including *cha soba,* which contains powdered green tea and has a green tinge; *nama soba,* containing egg and dusted with potato flour; and *zaru soba,* which is attractively speckled and contains yam. *Sobas* are eaten cold in the summer with a dipping sauce, or hot in a spicy broth.

Somen (Japanese) Fine white wheat-flour noodles similar to *hiya-mugi* but thinner. They are usually eaten cold, sometimes in a crystal bowl over ice, and garnished lightly with ginger or *shiso* with a dipping sauce on the side. There are a number of variations, including *cha somen* (with powdered green tea) and *tomago somen* (with egg yolk) They are sold dried.

Sorghum, juwar (Middle Eastern, African, Northern Chinese) An equally hardy relative of millet, and therefore a staple in marginal lands, sorghum is grown in the United States primarily as livestock food. Sometimes it's found in Indian groceries to use with wheat flour in making *rotis* and Sri Lankan *pittu.* It's also the base for the killer Chinese and Korean spirit *bhaegal.* There are two varieties of edible sorghum: it's the sweet one that makes the syrup still popular in parts of the American South; the other kind is used for flour.

Soursop, guanábana, corossol (Caribbean) The odd-looking fruit of a tropical American tree, *Annona muricata,* a less celebrated relative of the luscious custard apple. For looks, imagine a five-pound, spiny avocado. The white, pink, or yellow-orange custardy pulp is tart and delicately flavored. It's used mainly for drinks, ices, and sherbets, and is especially popular as a drink in Jamaica. Frozen soursop pulp and bottled drinks are sold in Latin American markets. A ripe soursop is soft on the outside, with no dark spots inside. Usually sold green, they will ripen in a few days when wrapped in a newspaper. They don't travel well but are sometimes sold, refrigerated, in ethnic markets.

RECIPE: **Soursop Drink**
From Ethlyn Hilton of Falmouth, Jamaica.

>1 large soursop
>water
>1 can sweetened condensed milk
>grated nutmeg

Peel soursop and chop flesh. Put in blender with just enough water to get it going. Purée, then add the condensed milk. Mix again, sprinkle with nutmeg, and serve.

Soybeans, daizu (Asian, Indian) One of the world's great protein sources, with the added benefit of enriching the soil on which it grows. They are sold whole and split, in black, yellow, green, and buff varieties, usually dried but sometimes fresh, and sometimes ground into grits. Soybeans are more commonly found metamorphosed into tofu, tempeh, miso, natto, soy sauce, and an array of other products than cooked and eaten plain. The beans are very hard and require long cooking, they are not digested as easily as fermented soy products, and they can be tricky to season effectively. Nevertheless I have eaten wonderful potato/soy curries, and I like fresh green soybeans, blanched before shelling and then popped out one by one and eaten with soy sauce.

RECIPE REFERENCE: **Beans and Assorted Vegetables,** *At Home with Japanese Cooking,* pp. 136–137.

Soy flour, kinako (Japanese) A pale yellowish flour made of dried soybeans. It goes rancid quickly, so buy it in small quantities and keep it refrigerated. It is sold roasted in Japanese markets, which takes care of its least attractive characteristic, a rather rank odor when raw.

Soy sauce, shoyu, tamari (Asian) A thin salty sauce of fermented soybeans, usually with other grains. National variations matter if you want your dish to have an authentic balance of flavor. The Japanese is the lightest in flavor and the least salty, especially if you choose a traditional brewed tamari, so when in doubt, use it. Better to underseason a dish than to overpower it. Japanese soy sauce also works well in Vietnamese dishes. Actually there are two major varieties of Japanese *shoyu*—light and dark. Light is lighter in color but also saltier. Both are lighter in flavor than standard Chinese soy sauce, which would overwhelm many Japanese dishes. Korean *kanjang* is similar to the medium-bodied Japanese varieties such as Kikkoman, which make a good substitute. Whatever type you buy, it's worth it to pay a bit more to get beyond the dirt-cheap, chemical-tasting, artificially colored ones. And at least once you should seek out a traditional, brewed, aged Japanese tamari (it's sold in bulk at our food co-op). The rich, complex flavor is a revelation. Many soy sauces include wheat; wheat-free varieties are available at natural foods stores. See also **Kecap manis**.

Spelt (European) An "unimproved" variety of wheat that grows well on marginal land and was common particularly in mountainous parts of Europe until well into the nineteenth century. Ancient Roman recipes include several for spelt soups and porridges. Nowadays it is found in natural foods stores and occasionally in Arabic markets. It does not differ markedly from hard whole-wheat flours.

Spicy tofu, soybean cakes, five-spice dry bean curd, doufu-gan (Chinese) Extra-firm tofu marinated in soy sauce and other spices, often including five-spice powder. They are dry and chewy and will keep for a week in the refrigerator (this is hearsay, as ours have never gone uneaten that long) or frozen for a couple of months. I used to work nights next door to a food co-op, and these were my standard dinner entrée. I never got as far as cooking with them, but they would surely be a good addition to many soups.

Squid (European, North African, Asian) Very popular in Asian and Mediterranean cuisines, squid are marketed frozen, canned, sun-dried, and pickled, as well as fresh. Sushi uses raw squid. Otherwise it is either fried very quickly—in Asian stir fries or Italian *fritti misti*—or given a long, slow cooking that takes it through the rubbery stage and beyond, as in the Italian dish *calamari in zimino*. Squid stuffed with rice is a common Mediterranean preparation. (The best example I ever had was actually on the Adriatic, in the then-Yugoslav town of Split.) *Calamares en su tinta*, the popular Spanish dish, is available canned. You can extract the ink for other recipes by pouring the can's contents through cheesecloth and squeezing out as much liquid as possible. The result will be oily, so skim off the top before mixing the ink with wine or water. Dried squid are often used in Chinese and Korean cooking. See **Dried scallops.**

Sriacha, Thai chile sauce (Thai) A combination of chiles, salt, sugar, and vinegar, similar to *sambal ulek,* but sweeter. Sold bottled in Asian markets and many supermarkets. See also **Sambal ulek.**

Star anise, aniz estrella (Asian, Latin American) A licorice-flavored spice used in five-spice powder and with Vietnamese beef. The beautiful, intricate seeds are worth having around just for looks.

Sufu, dofu-ru, fu yu (Japanese, Chinese) Wine-fermented tofu, similar in texture to a soft ripened cheese. Inoculated with mold and then ripened in a brine of rice wine, salt, red chiles, and other seasonings. Commonly this is mashed and then added to a vegetable stir-fry.

Sumac, Sumaq (North African, Middle Eastern) The berries from the common ornamental bush, sold in Middle Eastern markets, usually ground, sometimes whole. Whole berries must be cracked and soaked before use. Ground sumac, which is an attractive deep red, should be stored in an airtight jar as it loses its flavor rapidly. Sumac is much used in North Africa, both alone and as a crucial ingredient in *za'atar*. One of the famed dishes of medieval Baghdad was lamb simmered in sumac juice, and that combination of rich meat and tart juice remains popular. Sumac's flavor is sour but not sharp, and was used in Europe before the advent of the lemon. Mixed with chopped onion as a spice for roasts, or in vegetable salads. See also **Za'atar.**

———————— ❧ ————————

RECIPE: **Sumac Soup (Ash-e somaq)**
New Food of Life: Ancient Persian and Modern Iranian Cooking and Ceremonies, Najmieh Batmanglij, p. 74. *From Iran.*

> 3 cups and 1 tablespoon sumac powder
> 2 large onions, 1 peeled and thinly sliced, 1 peeled and grated
> 3 tablespoons oil
> 1 1/4 teaspoons salt
> 1/2 teaspoon freshly ground black pepper
> 1/2 teaspoon turmeric
> 2 cups rice
> 8 cups water
> 2 cups and 2 tablespoons chopped fresh parsley or 3/4 cup dried
> 2 cups chopped fresh coriander leaves or 1/2 cup dried
> 1 cup chopped fresh mint or 1/4 cup dried
> 1 cup chopped fresh tarragon or 1/4 cup dried
> 1 cup chopped fresh summer savoy or 1/4 cup dried
> 1/4 pound ground meat
> 1 tablespoon sugar (optional)

Garnish
2 tablespoons oil
5 cloves garlic, peeled and crushed
1 teaspoon dried mint
$^1/_2$ teaspoon turmeric

Cook 3 cups sumac in 6 cups of water for 35 minutes over medium heat. Drain through a strainer set over a bowl, reserving the sumac water.

In a heavy pot, brown the sliced onion in 3 tablespoons oil. Add 1 teaspoon salt, $^1/_4$ teaspoon pepper, $^1/_2$ teaspoon turmeric and rice. Sauté for a few minutes, then add 8 cups water.

Add herbs (except for 2 tablespoons of parsley) and the sumac water and simmer for 45 minutes longer. If using dried herbs, place a sieve in a bowl of lukewarm water and soak the dried herbs for 20 minutes. Remove the sieve from the bowl and use the herbs.

Combine the grated onion, meat, 2 tablespoons parsley, 1 tablespoon sumac powder, $^1/_4$ teaspoon salt, and $^1/_4$ teaspoon pepper. Mix ingredients thoroughly and shape into chestnut-size meatballs. Add to the pot and simmer for 1 hour 15 minutes.

Taste soup for seasoning—it should be both sweet and sour. Add sugar if the soup is too sour.

Just before serving, prepare the garnish. Heat 2 tablespoons oil in a skillet and brown the garlic. Remove from heat. Crumble the dried mint flakes in the palm of your hand and add to the garlic. Add the turmeric and mix well.

Pour the soup into a tureen and garnish with the mint, turmeric, and garlic mixture.

Note: For best results, make the *ash* a day in advance to give the flavors a chance to meld. Reheat it just before serving. Add the garnish after pouring the soup into the tureen. Serves 6.

————————— ❧ —————————

Sun mian (Chinese, Korean) Vermicelli-style noodles made of soft wheat.

Sweet red bean paste (Chinese, Japanese) A purée of Chinese red beans, sugar, and shortening—dark red, thick, and sweet. It is used in steamed pastries and sweet dishes and is sold in cans or by weight. In Canton, at least among affluent families, *hung bau* (red buns) made of dyed red steamed pastry filled with red bean paste, are traditionally given away to commemorate the birth of a baby girl.

❧ T ❧

Tahini (Middle Eastern, Chinese) Ground sesame paste used for falafel, hummus, and other dips. Very oily. Sold canned, bottled, and in tubs at Middle Eastern markets and many natural foods stores. The fresher the better, because if it sits it gets like old-fashioned peanut butter, where the solids sit in a lump on the bottom and resist any interaction with the oil on top. Chinese sesame paste is made of roasted seeds and is used in sauces. See **Sesame seeds,** p. 195.

Tamarind, asam, tamarindo (Indian, Southeast Asian, Latin American) The most popular souring agent in southern India and also essential to many Southeast Asian cuisines. Western diners who have experienced it only as one of the tastes in Worcestershire sauce are missing out. The podded fruit of the *Tamarindus indica* tree has a tangy taste that is milder than lemon, more flavorful than vinegar, and delightful in its many forms. Asian markets sell the pulp in blocks, and Indian markets sell a liquid concentrate, which should be diluted about 6 to 1. To use the blocks, soak a piece about 1-inch square in a cup of warm water for 20 minutes, then break apart the pulp and strain out the strings and seeds. Store the resulting liquid in the refrigerator, or you can freeze it for several months. Some Indonesian recipes ask you to take a chunk of tamarind paste and sear it in a dry skillet until slightly charred.

Tamarind is used primarily in sweets and cold drinks in Mexico and elsewhere in Latin America. Tamarind candies and soft drinks are popular in Asian, Indian-and-Latin American stores and have found their way to our local small-town supermarket. Lemon juice, mild vinegar, or sumac are possible substitutes, or if you can find them, tamarind slices (which aren't actually tamarind). See also **Sumac** and **Tamarind slices.**

RECIPE: Cauliflower and Potato Curry

This is one of our family favorites. You can do without the coconut milk, substituting some tomatoes to make up the liquid
and adding another potato to balance the increased acidity.

> One medium onion, chopped
> 6 tablespoons vegetable oil
> 3 dried red guajillo chiles or 2 teaspoons red pepper flakes
> 2 teaspoons coriander seeds
> $1/4$ teaspoon nigella seeds
> $1/4$ teaspoon fenugreek seeds
> $1/4$ teaspoon cumin seeds
> $1/2$ teaspoon ground cinnamon
> freshly ground pepper to taste
> $1/8$ teaspoon ground cloves
> $1/2$ teaspoon ground turmeric
> $1/2$ teaspoon paprika
> 1 heaping teaspoon tamarind paste
> $1/2$-inch ginger, peeled and chopped fine
> 4 garlic cloves, chopped fine
> 1 pound potatoes, peeled and chopped into large pieces
> salt
> 1 pound cauliflower, cut into large florets
> 13.5 oz. coconut milk

Heat 1 tablespoon of oil in a heavy skillet and sauté the onions
until soft. Set aside. Heat one more tablespoon of oil and sauté
the chiles, coriander seeds, nigella, fenugreek, and cumin seeds
briefly over medium-high heat. Put onion and cooked spices in

a blender or food processor. Add turmeric, paprika, and tamarind and $^1/_2$ cup water and purée. In a saucepan, heat remaining oil and sauté the ginger and garlic briefly. Add the puréed onions and spices, sauté for 2 minutes. Add the potatoes and a little water or tomato juice and sauté until potatoes are just starting to soften. Salt to taste. Add a bit more water and cook, covered, for about five minutes. Add more liquid if potatoes are starting to stick. Add the cauliflower and coconut milk and cook until done. Serves 4.

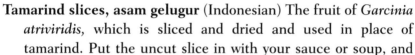

Tamarind slices, asam gelugur (Indonesian) The fruit of *Garcinia atriviridis,* which is sliced and dried and used in place of tamarind. Put the uncut slice in with your sauce or soup, and discard before serving. Tamarind slices are available in some Asian markets.

Tandoori masala (North Indian) The red spice mixture used to prepare meat and seafood for India's most famous restaurant dish. The premixed stuff is not comparable in flavor to making your own marinade, which is not difficult, but judging by the big bags of the stuff that I see in Indian groceries, a lot of restaurants are taking this shortcut. The bright red coloring that gives tandoori preparations their distinctive look is from a natural pigment called *tandoori rang.* I do not know its provenance. If it is unavailable, a mild sweet paprika makes an acceptable substitute.

RECIPE: Tandoori marinade
Classic Indian Cooking, p. 222. This recipe yields enough mari-nade for three small broiling chickens.

    2 large cloves garlic
    1 tablespoon fresh ginger root, chopped
    1 teaspoon ground roasted cumin seeds
    $1/2$ teaspoon ground cardamom
    $1/2$ teaspoon red pepper
    1 teaspoon *tandoori rang* or 1 tablespoon paprika
    $1/2$ cup plain yogurt

Mix all ingredients in blender or food processor. Rub over and into the chickens, which have been previously slashed all over and marinated 30 minutes with $1/3$ cup lemon juice mixed with $2^1/2$ teaspoons unseasoned meat tenderizer and let sit for at least 4 hours and up to 2 days. You won't get the exact texture without a tandoori oven, but this chicken will be delicious grilled or baked.

━━━━━━━━━━━━━━━

Tangerine peel, chenpi (Chinese, Japanese) The dried, intensely flavored peel of thin-skinned Asian tangerines is used to cut the richness of many braised and simmered Chinese dishes, especially with rich meats such as duck or mutton. Less common is its use to provide a bright bite to a stir fry. For slow-cooked dishes it can be added as is. For stir fries it's best to rehydrate first in rice wine. Dried orange peel is an acceptable, though not equivalent, substitute. It's easy to dry your own; start with organically grown fruit and you don't have to worry about pesticide residue on the skin.

RECIPE REFERENCE: Chicken with Broccoli and Citrus Peel, *Ken Hom's Asian Ingredients,* **pp. 110–111.**

Tang myon Korean buckwheat vermicelli, used in the noodle-and-vegetable favorite *chapchae.* Rice threads can be substituted.

Tapenade (European) A Provençal sauce featuring ground olives, anchovies, and capers. It is used as a dip for bread and is perhaps the world's best garnish for hash browns. *Tapenade* is sold in small, pricy bottles in most supermarkets these days, and, at restaurants, often cut with mayonnaise for economy. There are many variations on the basic theme. One California innovation adds salsa, lime juice, and chopped onions and finishes with a dollop of sour cream, but I don't think it's an improvement. My husband's favorite includes a can of tuna in the blend. My own preferred recipe is basic.

———————— ✑ ————————

RECIPE: Tapenade

> 2-ounce can of anchovies, rinsed
> $1/2$ cup California black olives
> $1/2$ cup Niçoise or other black, dry-cured olives
> $1/4$ cup capers
> $1/4$ cup good olive oil
> 1 tablespoon Dijon mustard

Blend everything, using more olive oil if necessary.

———————— ❧ ————————

Tapioca shreds, hu tieu uot (Chinese, Vietnamese) Noodles made of cassava, sold in big packages in Asian markets, sometimes dyed alarming colors. They are chewy but don't have much taste. They are used to provide texture to soft dishes such as the Vietnamese stew *kiem.*

RECIPE REFERENCE: **Squash and Sweet Potato Stew with Coconut and Peanuts (Kiem),** *The Simple Art of Vietnamese Cooking,* pp. 288–289.

Taro, cocoyam, gabi, coco, dasheen, eddo, baddo, malanga, tanier, tannia, yautia (Chinese, Japanese, Southeast Asian, Caribbean) Confusion reigns on the distinctions between these closely related species (*Colocasia antiquorum* and *Colocasia esculenta*), and common names are assigned more or less at random from country to country. The main botanical difference is that one species has a big central corm, or tuber, and a few side shoots, and the other has several smaller corms. Once the vegetables hit the market, though, these differences become immaterial. In general, these are all bland, starchy tubers, filling the same general culinary niche as cassava and true yam. The name under which you find them in recipes and stores will vary with the nationality. Herewith a brief tour: Taro belongs to the arum family and is known in Jamaica, Barbados, and Trinidad as *coco, eddo,* and *baddo,* the leaves being called *callaloo* and used in the eponymous and justly famous Caribbean soup. Also known as the "potato of the tropics," it is the main ingredient in

Hawaiian poi. It predates rice in some parts of Asia and is a staple in many peasant cuisines' meat dishes and stews, and also in desserts and pastes to fill *dim sum* confections. In Japanese cooking, small taros (called *gabi*) are used like new potatoes and sometimes translated as such in recipes—so a chicken or pork stew with miso and daikon may use little taros cut into bite-size pieces, which quickly cook to a smooth paste. Most Japanese groceries sell small taros for these uses, and I prefer them, for their convenient size and their slightly more interesting flavor, to cassava and yam. A closely related group, the malangas, also is cultivated in many of the Caribbean islands. These are sold in island markets as malanga, dasheen, tanier, tannia, and yautia. Their leaves are *also* known as callaloo. The dasheen that I bought in Jamaica was a homely, roundish root with a fibrous brown outside, chalky white within, with a slight acrid bite when raw. When boiled in chicken stock it was mild and a little sticky. Dasheen's flavor is sometimes described as similar to artichoke, but that wasn't how it struck me.

Tasajo (South American) Beef jerky below the equator, this is seasoned salt-cured beef, sun-dried and useful in places where refrigeration is not assured. It should be soaked before using in soups and casseroles.

Teff (African) A tiny, round, khaki-colored variety of millet, much touted in natural foods circles in recent years as one of the rediscovered grains of the ancient world. It is high in protein, drought-resistant, and not coincidentally the staple grain of Ethiopia, where it is used to make *injera*. Whole-grain *teff* and flour can be found in Middle Eastern markets and many natural foods stores. I like to add the flour to waffle batters, where it brings a nutty flavor and a crispier outside. Fine millet flour can be substituted for *teff* flour. See also **Injera.**

Tekka (Japanese) A concentrated condiment made of minced root vegetables such as burdock and turnips, cooked slowly with soybean miso. *Tekka* is sprinkled on grain dishes and used to make miso soup. One drawback to experimenting is that it's expensive and if you don't like it you'll have a lot left over. A sample-size bottle would be perfect but I have yet to see one.

Tempeh, tempe (Japanese, Indonesian) Boiled soybeans fermented with a special yeast, *Rhizopus oligosporus,* which improves digestibility and gives a nutty flavor to the resulting crumbly, protein-rich cake. In Java, which claims its invention, tempeh is burdened with the associations of a poverty food, something you ate when you couldn't have meat, while in North America it is most popular as a pricy item at natural foods stores, something to eat when you have evolved beyond meat. It is sold fresh or frozen, often flavored with various marinades or sauces and ready for the grill. Tempeh is always served cooked, either grilled or boiled separately, or crumbled into the other ingredients. Variations on tempeh can also be made with chickpeas, okara, peanuts (a Javanese specialty, called *oncom*) dried peas, rice, or wheat.

RECIPE REFERENCE: Spiced Tempe from Central Java (Botok Tempe), *Indonesian Regional Cooking,* pp. 168–169.

Tempura abura (Japanese) A mixture of vegetable oils used in deep-fat frying because it stays clear in color at high temperatures. It is sold in Japanese markets. You can substitute corn oil, peanut oil, or a combination vegetable oil such as Wesson.

Tentsuyu (Japanese) A sweet and salty dipping sauce for tempura, made from sweetened soy sauce, dashi, and *mirin*. It is not difficult to make but is also sold as a concentrate in Japanese markets for those times when speed matters more than top quality.

Tepín chile (Latin American) A very hot, round little chile, one of the indigenous varieties that are basically unchanged since prehistoric times. It's brick red when ripe; green ones are sometimes found pickled in Mexican markets. *Chile pequin* or *chile de árbol* can be substituted.

Thai basil, horapa, kemangi (Southeast Asian) Available in Asian groceries and farmers' markets, Thai basil has purple stems, relatively small leaves, and a somewhat sweeter taste and aroma than the European variety. It is well suited to the bright flavors of Southeast Asian cooking. Equal parts fresh European basil and fresh mint leaves make a fair substitute. Don't substitute dried leaves. The Indonesian herb *kemangi* is similar in flavor to the better-known Thai basil, and the two can be used interchangeably.

Thai eggplant, ca dai (Southeast Asian) These small, round eggplants range in size from a pea to a grapefruit, and in color from white to green, purple, yellow, and even red. Most Asian markets sell at least one type; they are often very beautiful. The milder-flavored ones can be eaten raw with a savory dip, as in the Javanese salad *Karedok*. (See **Asparagus bean** for recipe). The little green ones have a concentration of the bitter taste that a large eggplant just hints at, and are used by Thais and Laotians for sauces and green curries.

Thousand-year eggs, pine flower eggs, sung hwa don (Chinese, Southeast Asian) Duck eggs cured with salt, tea, and lime so that they can keep without refrigeration. These are sold in the shell, in soft and firm varieties. Usually the crust of muddy-looking lime in which they are preserved (for about two months, not a thousand years) is cleaned off, but not always. Inside they look weird; the white is gelatinous and stained amber by the tea, the yolk is a greenish mush. They are very salty, very rich, with a slight bite from the lime. The soft ones go in soup. The firmer ones may be sliced and served as a snack with a bit of pickled ginger, or used as a garnish for meat and vegetable dishes. A Southeast Asian version of salted egg must be cooked before using; it adds flavor to the traditional bland rice porridge *congee*. It's also used in moon cakes and other salty pastries.

Thua nao (Thai) The same soybean and bacterial culture as natto is mashed with salt, garlic, onion, and red pepper, wrapped in banana leaves, and cooked. The result is formed into small balls or chips and used as seasoning. See also **Natto.**

Tofu, doufu, tahu (Asian) The modern symbol for tasteless health food, tofu is actually one of the most versatile and ingenious of all staple ingredients, the "meat without bones" that for millennia has provided the protein needed in a rice-based diet. At its most basic, it is a mild-flavored, squishy-textured "cheese," made from soy milk and a souring ingredient. "The most usual, common and cheap sort of food all China abounds in, and which all in that Empire eat, from the Emperor to the meanest

Chinese," wrote Friar Domingo Navarrete in the seventeenth century, and he was a latecomer to a tradition already more than 1,500 years old.

That makes plenty of time for innovation, and tofu's variety in its major cuisines is now bewildering, with the recent additions of even more types for the North American health food trade. One good reference is *Tofu, Tempeh, and Other Soy Delights,* by William Shurtleff and Akiko Aoyagi, which covers both the traditional and New Age bases. See specific names.

Togarashi (Japanese) A small, hot, red chile available fresh and dried. Powdered *togarashi* is one of the ingredients in seven-spice powder. Serrano or red pepper flakes can substitute.

Tomatillo, mil tomate (Latin American) These are increasingly available fresh in supermarkets, as well as in Latin American groceries and farmers' markets. They are cousins to the cape gooseberry and to the garden ornamental Chinese lantern and, like them, grow inside a little papery husk. The fruit looks like a small green tomato and has a somewhat similar taste, though less acidic. They are also sold canned, with or without jalapeños, in Latin American groceries. Tomatillos are best known as the main ingredient in green salsas, but they also can be sautéed with onion and garlic to make a wonderful sauce for chicken or fish. Fresh ones have a slightly sticky coating under their husks. I wash mine in warm water with a touch of mild soap to get this off. If you don't find them in nearby stores, they are easy to grow and the attractive plants will reseed in your garden.

RECIPE: **Tomatillo Sauce**

I worked up this simple sauce when my garden produced too many tomatillos even for *salsa verde* fanatics such as ourselves. It freezes well, so it's fine to make in quantity.

> 4 cups tomatillos, husked and washed
> 1/2 teaspoon cumin seeds
> 1 medium onion, chopped
> 3 cloves garlic, minced
> 2 tablespoons vegetable oil
> 2 tablespoons chopped cilantro (optional)
> salt and freshly ground pepper to taste

Chop tomatillos into 1/2-inch chunks. Heat a heavy saucepan or medium skillet to medium-high. Add oil and cumin seeds and cook about 2 minutes. Reduce heat to medium-low and add onion and garlic. Cook gently until soft but not brown. Add tomatillos and cook about 15 minutes. Add salt and pepper to taste and sprinkle with cilantro (if used). This is divine over baked halibut or grilled chicken. Makes about 2 cups.

Totori muk, acorn curd (Korean) Slabs of gelatinous curd made from acorns. The flavor is bland, like tofu, and the uses are similar.

Tunas, cactus fruit (Mexican) The fruit of the nopal cactus is eaten fresh, either in salads or out of hand.

Tuong (Vietnamese) A thick bottled sauce made of fermented soybeans, sugar, and salt, used in dips and marinades. Similar to Javanese *kecap manis*. See also **Kecap manis.**

Turmeric, kunyit, kunir, nghe haldi (Indian, Indonesian, Vietnamese, Middle Eastern, North African) A smallish rhizome, usually used powdered as a coloring and base flavor in dals and curries. Also popular in the Arabian Gulf countries and in North Africa. Used as an inadequate substitute for saffron, where it provides a golden color but not saffron's haunting earth-and-flower flavor. Fresh turmeric root, sometimes available in natural foods stores, is worth trying, adding a delicate taste not found in the dried powder. Store the root whole, like ginger, and grate a bit off as needed. Slivers of it are used in Vietnamese stir fries, although, like lemongrass, it is not eaten but left on the plate.

Twoenjang, Korean soybean paste (Korean) Salty, chili-fired brown paste of fermented soybeans, ubiquitous in Korean cooking as a soup base and sauce flavoring. Japanese miso tends to be milder, but usable as a substitute in a pinch.

U

Ube, purple yam (Philippine) A bright purple tuber used to make Philippine puddings and jams. It is sold frozen and grated, or already prepared as jam in some Asian markets. The color is the most distinctive thing about it—that Day-Glo purple that my Sixties generation associates with the black lights at a psychedelic concert. The taste, like that of most true yams, is bland and starchy.

Udon (Japanese) Long, thick, squared-off noodles, made with soft wheat. It is used for hearty, not-too-refined snacks, and is available both fresh (*nama*) and dried. *Udon* makes good street fare, served with vegetables, fish sausage, *abura agé,* or tempura shrimp. You can freeze the fresh *udon* if it is truly fresh, not just defrosted. You can also make your own, preferably using the special flour blended for the purpose, labeled *"te uchi udon senyo komugiko."* The ingredients are simple: just flour, salt, and water. The preferred procedure is energetic, involving stamping on the dough with your bare feet for several minutes.

Ugli fruit (Caribbean) A cross between grapefruit and mandarin orange, grown primarily in Jamaica and referred to there as *"hoogli."* It is a bit ugly-looking, like a grapefruit with rumpled mandarinlike skin. The taste is likewise a blend, like a grapefruit with mandarin overtones. It's very refreshing on a hot day and wonderful in salads.

Umeboshi plums (Japanese) Small fruits, known as plums but actually a variety of apricot, generally pickled for a salty, sweet/sour taste, used as a snack or a condiment for Japanese dishes. They are available in many forms—a syruplike concentrate, vinegar, and paste, as well as whole. Brightly colored ones are suspect, as they are artificially colored. The more traditional ones are a softer pink, getting their coloring by being pickled along with a leaf of *aka-jiso.*

RECIPE REFERENCE: **Omusubi,** *At Home with Japanese Cooking,* pp. 80–81.

Urad dal, dhooli urad sabat ruad, maan, kali dal (Indian) Black gram beans favored in Delhi and also Punjabi cooking, generally combined with lots of ghee. They are sold both whole and black (*kali dal*), or skinned and split (*urad dal*), which yields a quick-cooking, dusty white legume. *Urad dal* are soaked and ground and then combined with rice flour to make the divine sourdough pancakes called *dosa,* India's answer to Ethiopian *injera. Urad dal* is also roasted and ground for *papadum* and to add to spice mixtures and chutneys.

———————————— ✌ ————————————

RECIPE: **Dosa**

These pancakes are easy to make, but you need to allow time for soaking and fermentation. You could mix them up in the evening, leave out overnight, and then refrigerate the batter until dinnertime.

> 1 cup urad dal, soaked 8 hours in warm water
> about 4 cups of water
> 2 cups plus one tablespoon rice flour (do not use
>   glutinous rice flour)
> salt
> vegetable oil

Drain dal, reserving liquid. Place in blender, add one cup of the soaking liquid and blend into a smooth paste. Add more water if needed.

Mix the 2 cups of rice flour with the dal, salt, and 2 cups of water and stir to make a thick batter. Let rest while you heat $1/2$ cup of water in a small saucepan. Stir in the remaining tablespoon of rice flour and cook until it begins to thicken. Remove from heat and stir until mixture cools to lukewarm. Add to batter and stir until thoroughly blended. Cover the bowl and let rest at least 6 hours at room temperature. The batter will be bubbly, with a tangy sourdough aroma when it's ready.

Cook dosa on a lightly oiled skillet over medium-high heat. The batter should be thin enough to pour easily and make a crepelike pancake. Add a bit more water if necessary. Cook on the first side until it bubbles and solidifies enough to turn over, about 2 minutes. Turn and cook about another minute. Stack finished dosa and cover with a towel until ready to serve. Makes about twenty 8-inch pancakes.

V

Varak (Indian) Edible silver (or gold) leaf used on Indian rice dishes and pastries. It does have a slightly metallic taste, but the symbolism is certainly more important than the flavor. The sheets are stored between two sheets of tissue paper and must be protected from tarnish, since they can't be polished.

Vinegar Like liquor, vinegar can be made of just about anything from the vegetable kingdom, and it can range from exquisite to rotgut. Many traditional cooks make their own—in Mexico commonly of pineapple—and count on their particular flavors to bring a recipe alive. The exact type is not essential to most dishes, but it's important to be in the ballpark. Sushi made with a sharp cider vinegar just isn't the same.

Black rice vinegar (Chinese) Made from glutinous "sweet rice," this is China's answer to balsamic vinegar, with a similar dark color and a rich, mild taste. It is used for braising.

Red rice vinegar (Chinese) Clear, pink, sweet/tart, and salty. It is used for dipping.

Sweet rice vinegar (Chinese) Brownish black and caramelized, with a slight licorice flavor from star anise. It doesn't have much vinegar taste.

White rice vinegar (Chinese, Japanese) Clear and mild with the rice flavor hovering around the edges. It is used for sweet and sour dishes, and is also sold sweetened and spiced. Some varieties are flavored especially for sushi.

Turkish vinegar Strong and sharp, but with a touch of sweetness. It is important for *tarators*. You can approximate its taste by combining wine and balsamic vinegars.

Balsamic vinegar (Italian) The real thing is made from the essence of Trebbiano grape skins and aged for ten years and more in a series of casks of different woods. The result is complex, mellow, and fabulously expensive. The merely pricy grocery store versions are not the same, but they still make it tough to go back to your basic red wine vinegar.

Palm vinegar (Asian) A mild white vinegar popular in the Philippines, where it is used to flavor adobo.

Cuka (Indonesian) A colorless vinegar used in Indonesian cooking. Distilled malt vinegar is the best substitute.

❧ W ❧

Wakame (Japanese) A seaweed similar to the better-known nori but with a clear green color. It is sold dried but is often reconstituted before adding to rice, salads, and pickles. It is often served in breakfast miso soups.

Warka (North African, Middle Eastern) A round, thin, translucent pastry leaf, used in Moroccan cooking, including the famous *bastilla* (pigeon pie). *Filo* is a common substitute, though crisper and drier. Round egg-roll wrappers found in Asian groceries and many supermarkets are thicker, but come close to approximating the texture.

Wasabi (Japanese) This is the innocent-looking green condiment that sits beside your sushi and sashimi and then makes your eyes water. True wasabi is a wild horseradish from the Japanese mountains. Few North Americans have ever tasted the real thing, as the total supply is not enough to satisfy demand in good Japanese restaurants. Some growers are attempting cultivation, and I wish them well, as the taste is supposed to be brighter and less harsh than regular horseradish, a better complement to the subtle tastes of sashimi. Most U.S. "wasabi" is simply regular horseradish or at best a mixture of the two, dyed green. It is available in tubes and powdered. Kaiseki brand is guaranteed to be actual wasabi, however, and is correspondingly expensive.

Water chestnuts (Chinese) Sometimes sold fresh in Asian markets, they are crunchy and much sweeter than the familiar canned ones—worth seeking out. They are shaped like a chestnut with a purple-brown peel that must be removed before eating. Fresh ones should be hard all over, with no soft spots indicating age. The freshest and best should be eaten raw so you will know what the real thing is supposed to taste like. They also are used in stir fries and soups, and sometimes cooked in a sugar syrup as a sweet treat. A powder made of dried, ground water chestnuts is used to make satiny sauces and also the *dim sum* given here.

RECIPE REFERENCE: **Water Chestnut Cake,** *The Dim Sum Book,* p. 144.

Water spinach, ong choi, pak-boong, kangkung, swamp cabbage (Indonesian, Vietnamese, Thai) A green, smooth-leafed water plant, milder than spinach, which is often used as a substitute in Western kitchens. The tender leaves are arrowhead shaped and the stems, left on for cooking, provide an interesting crunchy contrast. It is popular in stir fries, and barely cooked in soups.

RECIPE REFERENCE: **Water Spinach Sauté (Rau Muong Xao Chao),** *The Simple Art of Vietnamese Cooking,* p. 291.

Wheat berries, jareesh, habhab, dzedzadz, gorgod, Asurelik bugday (North African, Middle Eastern) Whole-wheat kernels were one of the first foods of agriculture, and they still are popular in Middle Eastern cooking. The small, plump grains are available unhulled or hulled in Arab markets and in natural foods stores. If your association, like mine, is from sink-like-a-rock casseroles from the early natural foods period, it's worth checking out cuisines that have had centuries of practice. Wheat berries require long cooking and have a chewy, slightly sweet flavor that goes well with sweet spices. The famous Bedouin soup *shorait habhab,* "the soup of tiny round pieces," uses wheat berries along with cinnamon, cardamom, lamb, garlic, and onions, while the Turkish dessert *asure,* which is supposed to have first been made by Noah and his family with the last food available on the ark, uses sweet dried fruit and rose water. Egyptians cook the grains with chicken in a popular dish called *ferique.*

RECIPE REFERENCE: **Asure,** *Classical Turkish Cooking,* p. 230.

White poppy seeds (Indian) The taste is similar to that of the more familiar black ones, so the main difference is in the visual effect. White seeds are toasted and ground to use as a thickening agent in Moghul and Hyderabad dishes and in Muslim Indian cuisines. They are sold in Asian markets. They don't keep as well as black ones; those not used immediately should be refrigerated.

Wine-sediment paste (Chinese) A red seasoning made from fermented rice and rice wine sediments, particularly popular in Fukien, where it is used with chicken and shellfish.

RECIPE REFERENCE: **Stir-Fried Lobster with Red Wine-Sediment Paste,** *The Encyclopedia of Chinese Cooking,* pp. 292–293.

Winter melon, tung kwa (Chinese) Not a melon but a green squash (*Benincasa hispida*) shaped about like a large pumpkin, with a waxy whitish coating reminiscent of snow—hence the name. It has rather soft flesh and a mild, slightly sweet flavor that blends well with more savory ingredients and is also valued in the mild soups favored in Cantonese cooking. It is sold canned and fresh in Chinese markets.

Wooster sosu (Japanese) A dark, spicy version of Worcestershire sauce, popular with pork, and available in Japanese groceries.

RECIPE REFERENCE: **Yaki Soba,** *At Home with Japanese Cooking,* p. 106.

Wu pei, fresh bean-curd skin (Chinese) Sometimes labeled "spring roll pastry," but distinguished from spring roll skins by their size (about two feet in diameter) and yellow-brown color, these are fresh sheets of the skimmed skin off soy milk. It is sold refrigerated or frozen in Asian markets. Cantonese cookbook author Eileen Yin-Fei Lo recommends that you ask for them by their Cantonese name, *wu pei,* to avoid confusion. Once thawed, these skins will keep about two weeks in a tightly closed container in the refrigerator, but they get brittle right away in the open air, so keep them covered as you work. They are used to make vegetable rolls and other *dim sum* and to simulate poultry skin (and fat) in dishes. See also **Yuba.**

RECIPE REFERENCE: **Vegetarian Goose (Jai Sui Ngaw),** *From the Earth: Chinese Vegetarian Cooking,* p. 193.

❧ X, Y, Z ❧

Xoi gat, carrot powder (Vietnamese) A bright orange powder (made from a dried fruit, not from carrots) and used in tiny quantities to color rice in festive dishes such as orange wedding rice. It is sometimes available in Asian markets or herb stores.

Yaki (Japanese) Flame-broiled tofu, charred on the outside, moist on the inside.

Yam, camote, ñame (African, Caribbean, Asian) This is the true yam, a big starchy root, and not the sweet potato variant of American Thanksgivings. It is native to tropical America and a staple of the native diet before European contact. The plant is a vine. The part you eat is the tuber, which can weigh up to twenty pounds, though the ones sold in markets are much smaller. They have a thick, rough skin, hairy and usually dark brown. Inside is a dense white and sometimes reddish fibrous material that is rich in carbohydrate, particularly starch.

Pounded into paste or dried to powder, it is used to make *fufu,* the ubiquitous West African carbohydrate. In the Caribbean it is boiled, baked, fried, and pounded into meal. In the cultures that depend upon it, it fills the role of rice, mashed potato, biscuits, or poi—a bland, abundant dish that fills you up and also absorbs flavor. Yam is now available in African markets as a powdered instant—just add water—imported from Nigeria.

——————— ❧ ———————

RECIPE: **Frituras de Ñame**

From the Dominican Republic. The Cooking of the Caribbean Islands, p. 72.

1 pound fresh yams, peeled and finely grated
1 tablespoon butter, melted and cooled
1 tablespoon onion, finely grated
1 tablespoon fresh parsley, finely chopped
1 $^1/_2$ teaspoons salt
freshly ground black pepper
2 egg yolks
$^1/_4$ cup vegetable oil

Combine yams, butter, onion, parsley, salt, and pepper, and mix well. Drop in egg yolks and beat vigorously with a large spoon until mixture is fairly smooth and thick enough to come away from the sides in an almost solid mass.

Line a large, shallow baking dish with paper towels and place in the oven. Preheat to lowest setting. In a large, heavy skillet, heat oil over medium heat until a light haze forms above it. For each cake, drop about a tablespoon of yam mixture in hot oil. Cook 4 or 5 at a time, leaving space between so they can spread into 2- to 2$^1/_2$-inch rounds. Fry cakes about 4 minutes on each side, or until golden and crisp around the edges. Transfer to the lined dish to drain and keep warm. Serve at once. Makes twenty 2-inch-round cakes.

———————— ☙ ————————

Yee tow, swim bladder (Chinese) The Chinese appreciation of contrasting textures in food, combined with a tradition of wasting nothing, makes for some rather peculiar ingredients, and this is one. It's the air sac a deepwater fish uses to raise and lower itself. Available dried in Chinese markets, it is tan colored and comes in curved pieces. Soak it in cold water 3–4 hours and it will expand to 3 times its original size. Drain and blot dry. Then it can be diced for use in soup or stir-fry meat dishes, or deep fried, which makes it puff up into a sort of light marine dumpling.

Yellow bean sauce (Chinese, Thai) Salted, preserved yellow soy beans, often sold canned in liquid. Sichuan and Hunan versions have chiles added, while Thai brands are likely to contain more salt. Use it in stir fries and to flavor Peking duck.

Yokan (Japanese) A prepared sweet sold in Japanese delicatessens. It combines agar gelatin with sweetened bean paste and other flavorings.

Yuba, tau hu ky, dried bean-curd skin (Asian) Originally Chinese, but also popular in Japan and Vietnam. The creamy film that forms on heated soy milk is scooped up to stretch and dry in sheets or rolls. They are sold completely dry and brittle, labeled "dried bean curd" or "bean sticks." They are soaked and then used to make mock meat dishes known as *Buddha's Duck* and *Buddha's Chicken,* and even *Buddha's Goose Skin.* Other uses include crumbling pieces into soup, steaming with vegetables, or frying until crispy and sprinkling on rice or stir fries. See also **Wu pei.**

Yuzu (Japanese) A small citrus fruit sometimes available in Japanese markets. It is sour, with a distinctive aroma, and is valued primarily for its rind, which is used both as flavoring and as a decorative garnish.

Zambo chile (Latin American) A Central American favorite similar to the *Coban* chile. Zambos are about two inches long, red, broad and medium-hot. They are sold dried.

Za'atar, zahtar (North African, Middle Eastern) *Za'atar* is the Arabic word for thyme, and Middle Eastern stores may sell plain thyme as *za'atar* and the eponymous spice mixture as black *za'atar.* Or the mixture may be labeled plain *za'atar,* so look and sniff before you buy. *Za'atar* the spice mixture contains sumac and dried thyme and may also have chickpea powder, sesame seeds, marjoram, and salt. You can make your own according to your taste. The sumac gives an acidic tang, while the thyme and other herbs take the taste in the direction of *herbes de provence.* *Za'atar* is a spice mixture used in meat balls or vegetables, mixed with olive oil and brushed over bread before baking, added to olives and olive oil, served with yogurt or olives, and used, by me, on roast potatoes and with great acclaim as a replacement for the traditional dill in a Russian vegetable pie, so it goes well with cabbage. See also **Sumac.**

RECIPE: **Vegetable Pie**
Modified from the *Winter Harvest Cookbook,* p. 112.

Pastry
1 1/4 cups flour
1 teaspoon salt
2 tablespoons butter
4 ounces cream cheese

Sift together flour and salt. Cut in butter until mixture is the size of peas. Work in cream cheese and roll pastry into two balls, one twice as big as the other. Chill until vegetables are ready. Then roll out the bigger ball and line a 9- or 10-inch pie pan. Roll out the remaining ball for the top crust.

Filling
4 tablespoons oil, divided
3 cups shredded green or red cabbage (one small cabbage)
1 medium onion, chopped
2 cups sliced mushrooms
salt and pepper
1 1/2 teaspoons za'atar
4 ounces softened cream cheese

Preheat oven to 400 F. Heat 2 tablespoons of the oil in a large skillet or saucepan. Add cabbage and onion and sauté for 10 minutes. Heat remaining 2 tablespoons of oil in another skillet or pan. Add mushrooms, salt, pepper, and za'atar and sauté for 5 minutes.

Spread cream cheese in bottom of pie shell. Spread cabbage and onion mixture evenly over cream cheese and follow with mushrooms. Cover with top crust. Make some decorative cuts in the top crust. Bake 15 minutes at 400, reduce heat to 350, and bake another 20 to 25 minutes. Cool a few minutes before serving. Serves 6 to 8.

———————— ✌ ————————

Zenryu-fu, wheat gluten (Japanese, Chinese) An invention of vegetarian Buddhist monks, who came up with an array of mock meats from wheat and soy. Made from gluten, it is used like a dumpling in soups or served with sauce. It is sold refrigerated or canned in Asian markets, sometimes already fried in a spicy mixture and ready to use. The flavor is bland, and is basically a sponge for other tastes. The texture is a bit rubbery, as you'd expect from gluten.

RECIPE REFERENCE: **Stir-fried Vegetarian Wheat Gluten,** *Ken Hom's Asian Ingredients,* p. 135.

Recommended Books

———————— ॐ ————————

I like ethnic cookbooks that combine fairly simple, home-oriented recipes with a bit of armchair traveling. These are some of my favorites.

The Africa News Cookbook: African Cooking for Western Kitchens. Africa News Service, edited by Tami Hultman. 1985. New York: Penguin Books.
A quick survey of African cooking, from Morocco to Capetown, with particular attention to accessible, delicious seafood and poultry recipes. It contains an interesting shortcut to making *injera*.

The Arabian Delights Cookbook: Mediterranean Cousins from Mecca to Marrakech. Anne Marie Weiss-Armush. 1994. Los Angeles: Lowell House.
A fascinating, beautifully presented collection of recipes and techniques from the Maghred (North Africa), the Levant (Lebanon, Syria, Jordan, and the Palestinians), and the Ara-

bian peninsula (Saudi Arabia, UAE, Bahrain, Kuwait, Oman, and Qatar). The author married into a Syrian family and has made it a mission to bring the sophisticated and little-known cuisines of the Arab world to tables in Western homes.

The Art of Mexican Cooking: Traditional Mexican Cooking for Aficionados. Diana Kennedy. 1989. New York: Bantam. The fifth of Kennedy's magnificent books on Mexican cuisines. They make me ache with nostalgia for the tastes and smells of my childhood Mexican sojourn. Mexican cuisine brings amazing variations to the most basic ingredients. This book contains sensible information on doing it yourself, with a concern for authenticity, but takes a reasonable approach to substitutions.

At Home with Japanese Cooking. Elizabeth Andoh. 1980. New York: Knopf.
A great ingredients list and very clear recipes with lots of regional variety. Andoh married into a traditional Japanese family and has studied Japanese cooking seriously for many years.

The Book of Latin American Cooking. Elisabeth Lambert Ortiz. 1979. New York: Knopf.
A straightforward selection that does reasonable justice to the many types of Latin American cooking. The book has a great glossary and wonderful Brazilian recipes.

The Burmese Kitchen: Recipes from the Golden Land. Copeland Marks and Aung Thein. 1987. New York: M. Evans and Co.

Weird and wonderful recipes from one of the most inventive cuisines on earth, now largely inaccessible to tourists. Great uses of shrimp paste.

The Cheese Book. Vivienne Marquis and Patricia Haskell. 1985 (revised edition). New York: Simon and Schuster.
Great bedside reading; a literate, appreciative, discriminating introduction and celebration of cheese. If you are studying a particular European cuisine, dive in to this essential supplement.

The Chestnut Cook Book. Annie Bhagwandin. 1996. Onalaska, WA: Shady Grove Publications.
A small treasure, this little book gives an international approach to one of the Americas' least-known "important foods." The author and her husband run a chestnut mail-order business, selling hard-to-find chestnut flour as well as dried nuts.

Classic Indian Cooking. Julie Sahni. 1980. New York: Morrow.
The best general introduction to Indian cooking I have read. Clear explanations of the basics—a simple dal, the cooking of basmati rice—and a splendid array of recipes.

Classical Turkish Cooking: Traditional Turkish Food for the American Kitchen. Ayla Algar. 1991. New York: HarperCollins.
Turkish food is one of the great crossroads cuisines, with Mediterranean, central Asian, and Arabic influences. Some of the best food I have ever cooked has come from this book.

The Complete Book of Caribbean Cooking. Elisabeth Lambert Ortiz. 1973. New York: Ballantine.
A huge variety of cuisines and styles are represented here, from colonial (stuffed Edam cheese) to African to Amerindian to Latin American to French. Recipes are clearly presented and unfamiliar ingredients explained. It's a good way to get a feel for the many influences and the tremendous variety of island approaches to cooking.

Cuisine of the Sun: Classical French Cooking from Nice and Provence. Mireille Johnston. 1976. New York: Random House.
Sensuous writing and intriguing dishes woven with the author's childhood in Nice. This is a wonderful book.

The Dim Sum Book: Classic Recipes from the Chinese Teahouse. Eileen Yin-Fei Lo. 1982. New York: Crown.
Lucid explanations and drawings demystify the delights of dim sum.

Dishes from Indonesia. Yohanni Johns. 1971. West Melbourne, Australia: Thomas Nelson Ltd.
This book features an encouraging introduction by the author, who has spent a lifetime interpreting her native cuisine to foreigners as a wife and a cooking teacher. Includes an excellent explanation of the cooking properties of coconut.

The Encyclopedia of Chinese Cooking. Kenneth Lo. 1979. New York: Exeter Books.
Two of this tome's strong points are its lucid explanation of the basics of Chinese cooking techniques—the combina-

tions of braising and frying and steaming that go together to produce particular flavors and textures—and the author's explanations of how and why Chinese restaurant food in other countries differs from that served in Chinese homes and at banquets. The heavy reliance on MSG dates the book, but the recipes are good without it.

False Tongues and Sunday Bread: A Guatemalan and Mayan Cookbook. Copeland Marks. 1985. New York: M. Evans and Co.
A comprehensive combination of the food and history of Central America. Besides the recipes, it presents a sort of culinary atlas of cultural influences on food, from the indigenous ingredients and techniques of the Indian highlands of Guatemala to the Europeanized cuisine of Guatemala City and Costa Rica, for example, and the Caribbean influence of eastern Nicaragua. Many recipes are closely related and show the variations that develop in isolated villages. This book also gives full representation to the famous Central American sweet tooth—many fritters, dumplings, and other syrupy dishes.

Fire & Spice: The Cuisine of Sri Lanka. Heather Jansz Balasuriya and Karin Winegar. 1989. New York: McGraw Hill.
A guide to the hottest and one of the most complex of the "curry" cuisines. It's written by a restaurateur, and the dishes are correspondingly skewed away from home cooking, but it contains recipes and techniques I have not seen elsewhere.

First Catch Your Eland. Laurens van der Post. 1978. New York: Morrow.
A fascinating combination of travel, history, and food, infused with a bit of the white man's burden. Van der Post is eloquent on both the arrogance of the standard colonial approach to food in Africa, and the magnificent cooking that results when the cultures combine forces.

Flatbreads and Flavors: A Baker's Atlas. Jeffrey Alford and Naomi Duguid. 1995. New York: Morrow.
Bread is the heart of cuisine, nearly everywhere, and flatbreads are the basis of rural and nomadic cooking on most continents. This book takes some time to sort out, arranged as it is by culture rather than by course, but it is wonderful.

Flavours of Korea. Marc and Kim Mellon. 1991. London: Andre Deutsch.
Family recipes, reminiscences, and travel diaries by the grandson of a noted Korean cook, charmingly illustrated.

The Food and Cooking of Eastern Europe. Lesley Chamberlain. 1989. New York: Viking Penguin.
The author expertly picks out the cultural and historic influences of this tangled area and presents them in a well-chosen series of recipes.

Food in History. Rhea Tannahill. 1973. Briarcliff Manor, NY: Scarborough House.
Reads like a whodunit; an enthralling tale of the spread of various foods and traditions from prehistoric times through the late twentieth century.

Food in Tibetan Life. Rinjing Dorje. 1985. London: Prospect Books.
A fascinating look at a little-known culture and a style of cooking that has long had to make the most out of slim materials. It includes information on Tibetan religious and cultural traditions, medicine, and social life.

From the Earth: Chinese Vegetarian Cooking. Eileen Yin-Fei Lo. 1995. New York: Macmillan.
The author's family reminiscences help place her 200 recipes in the context of Chinese food traditions. Classic dishes are included along with Yin-Fei Lo's own inventions and adaptations.

From the Land of Figs and Olives. Habeeb Salloum and James Peters. 1995. New York: Interlink Books.
More than 300 mostly simple, accessible recipes.

The Great Book of Couscous: Classic Cuisines of Morocco, Algeria and Tunisia. Copeland Marks. 1994. New York: Donald I. Fine.
Unusual in that it focuses on the Jewish cuisines of these primarily Muslim countries. Its organization is a bit frustrating, but it is an excellent resource.

The Great Curries of India. Camilla Panjabi. 1995. New York: Simon and Schuster.
Gorgeous and wide-ranging. This is a good reference for ingredients and regional styles, but it tends toward the verbose.

Indonesian Regional Cooking. Sri Owen. 1994. New York: St. Martin's Press.

A fascinating, erudite, and discriminating discussion of Indonesian food traditions and modern cooking styles by a world authority on Indonesian food, and it has great recipes, too. This book is an important contribution to anyone's food/anthropology library.

Japan: The Beauty of Food. Reinhart Wolf; text by Angela Terzani-Staude. 1987. New York: Rizzoli.

An art book, not a cookbook. It provides a visual reference and esoteric information for many traditional Japanese dishes and has sublimely beautiful pictures.

Ken Hom's Asian Ingredients: A Guide with Recipes. Ken Hom. 1996. Berkeley, CA: Ten Speed Press.

Just what the title says.

A Mediterranean Harvest. Poala Scaravelli and Jon Cohen. 1986. New York: E.P. Dutton.

One of my favorite cookbooks. Contains little known Provencal, Spanish, and Italian recipes as well as Turkish and North African ones. Recipes are for seafood and vegetables only—no red meat or chicken.

On Food and Cooking: The Science and Lore of the Kitchen. Harold McGee. 1984. New York: Charles Scribner's Sons.

Not a cookbook, though it has some recipes. This is the place to find out why mayonnaise emulsifies, or the chemical reason why many vegetables lose color when cooked, or to see with an electron microscope photo why durum wheat makes pasta and soft wheat makes pie crust. Fascinating.

Philippine Recipes Made Easy. Violeta A. Noriega. 1993. Kirkland, WA: Paperworks.
This book lives up to its name and deserves wider distribution; it contains simple, well-organized recipes and descriptions of culinary influences and the Philippine table.

The Rice Book. Sri Owen. 1993. New York: St. Martin's Press.
An examination of the agricultural and cultural significance of rice, and a collection of carefully tested recipes from around the world and from the author's own kitchen. A tour de force that won the James Beard Award.

The Simple Art of Vietnamese Cooking. Binh Duong and Marcia Kiesel. 1991. New York: Prentice-Hall Press.
This collection by a well-known restaurateur and a New York food writer is clearly written and nicely chosen. The authors' trip to Vietnam during its research adds a depth of information and association.

Southeast Asian Cooking. California Culinary Academy, Jay Harlow. 1987. San Francisco: Ortho Information Services.
A nice survey of Southeast Asian cuisines, with clear information on ingredients and techniques, and terrific recipes.

A West African Cookbook. by Ellen Gibson Wilson. 1971. New York: M. Evans and Co.
A useful compilation of food from Ghana, Nigeria, Sierra Leone, and Liberia. The author, wife of a British diplomat

in Africa, was one of the first to research and publicize the influence of West African food on American Southern cooking. The book includes both village recipes and many from the educated urban elite, with more Western ingredients and European techniques combined with traditional ones.

Winter Harvest Cookbook. Lane Morgan. 1990. Seattle: Sasquatch Books.

My first food book, this selection of recipes using fresh winter produce was a chance to marry my research into ethnic food with my love of gardening.

Index

Merguez, 132
Mesclun, 132–33
Mesticanza, 132–33
Methi, 92–93
Mexican cuisine, 17–18
Middle Eastern cuisine, 36
Middle Eastern green olives, 147
Mil tomate, 203
Mirasól, 105
Mirin, 133
Mirliton, 69–70
Miso, 133
Mit, 62–63
Mlookheeyeh, 134–35
Mochi, 133–34
Mochi-gomé, 102–3
Mogi posot, 76
Mo kwa, 98
Mole, 134
Molokhia, 134–35
Momo, 110
Mon go, 128–29
Mongo, 136
Monkey bread, 52–53
Mooli lobahk, 82–83
Moong dal, 136
Moqueca de Peixe (recipe), 161
Moroccan Carrot Salad (recipe), 159
Moroccan dry-cured olives, 158
Moroccan olives, 147
Mugi cha, 135
Mugwort, 135
Muligapuri, 135
Mung beans, 136
Muscoli, 136–37
Mussel and Needle Soup (recipe
  reference), 137
Mussels, 136–37
Mustard green, 137

Mustard oil, 137
Mutant gelatinous coconut, 127

Naeng myun, 137
Naflion olives, 146
Ñame, 214
Naméko, 137
Nam padek, 96–97
Nam pla, 143
Nar, 162
Nar suyu, 162
Naseberry, 137–38
Nasi Gurih (recipe), 104
Natto, 138
Neem, 82
Nepalese cuisine, 35
New Potatoes with Bzar (recipe reference),
  60
Ngapi Phoke (recipe), 200
Ngau yuk siu mai, 86
Nghe haldi, 205
Ngo gai, 92
Niçoise olives, 146
Nigella, 138
Nitter kibbeh, 138–39
Nitter Kibbeh (recipe), 139–40
Nixtamal, 140
Nohut, 99
Noodles, 140–42
Nopales, 142–43
Nopales en Blanco (recipe reference), 143
Nori, 143
Nor mai, 87
North African cuisine, 36–38
North African Beet Salad (recipe), 148
Nuoc mam, 143
Nyon olives, 146

Okara, 144